QUEBEC CITY
TRAVEL GUIDE 2025-2026

An Extensive Exploration of the City's History, Timeless Beauty, Majestic Architecture, Outdoor Activities and Vibrant Culture in One of Canada's Most Captivating Destinations.

ALL RIGHTS RESERVED

No part of this publication by **MICHAEL C GATES** may be reproduced, distributed, or transmitted in any form or by any means, including photocopying, recording, or other electronic or mechanical methods, without the prior written permission of the publisher, except in the case of brief quotations embodied in critical reviews and certain other noncommercial uses permitted by copyright law.

DISCLAIMER

This travel guide is intended for informational purposes only. While every effort has been made to ensure accuracy, travel conditions, regulations, and services may change. Readers should verify important details such as visa requirements, safety guidelines, and local laws with official sources before traveling.

The author and publisher assume no responsibility for any losses, injuries, or inconveniences resulting from the use of this guide. Travelers are encouraged to exercise caution, use their best judgment, and adhere to local laws while exploring.

Any recommendations for businesses, activities, or services are based on research and opinions and do not imply endorsement. Always check with trusted sources for the latest updates before making travel decisions.

TABLE OF CONTENT

Chapter 1. Introduction to Québec City — 4
    1.1 Overview of the City — 4
    1.2 Why Visit Québec City in 2025–2026 — 5
    1.3 Brief History & Cultural Significance — 8

Chapter 2. Getting to and Around Québec City — 12
    2.1 Arrival: Airports, Trains & Buses — 12
    2.2 Public Transport, Taxis & Ride-Sharing — 15
    2.3 Renting a Car or Bike — 19

Chapter 3: Top Attractions in Québec City — 24
    3.1 Old Québec (Vieux-Québec) – UNESCO Site — 24
    3.2 Château Frontenac — 28
    3.3 Montmorency Falls Park (Parc de la Chute-Montmorency) — 32
    3.4 Plains of Abraham & The Citadel — 36
    3.5 Quartier Petit Champlain — 40
    3.6 Musée de la Civilisation — 44
    3.7 Basilica of Sainte-Anne-de-Beaupré — 48

Chapter 4. Best Accommodation Options — 53
    4.1 Luxury Hotels & Historic Inns — 53
    4.2 Mid-Range Hotels & Boutique Stays — 56
    4.3 Budget-Friendly Lodgings — 60
    4.4 Unique Stays: B&Bs, Cabins & Apartment Rentals — 63

Chapter 5. Food & Drink in Québec City — 68
    5.1 Traditional Québécois Cuisine — 68
    5.2 Top Restaurants & Local Favorites — 72
    5.3 Best Cafés, Bistros & Bakeries — 76

Chapter 6. Festivals & Events — 81
    6.1 Winter Carnival (Carnaval de Québec) — 81
    6.2 Summer Festivals & Outdoor Shows — 84
    6.3 Cultural & Art Events — 88
    6.4 Holiday Markets & Seasonal Celebrations — 92

Chapter 7. Outdoor Activities & Day Trips — 97
    7.1 Cycling & Riverfront Trails — 97
    7.2 Skiing, Snowshoeing & Ice Activities — 101
    7.3 Day Trips: Île d'Orléans, Wendake & Le Massif — 106

Chapter 8. Arts, History & Culture — 110
    8.1 Museums & Historic Sites — 110
    8.2 Local Artists & Galleries — 115
    8.3 French-Canadian Heritage & Traditions — 119

Chapter 9. Shopping & Souvenirs — **125**
   9.1 Best Shopping Streets & Local Markets — 125
   9.2 Québec-Made Products & Crafts — 129
   9.3 Fashion, Boutiques & Antique Finds — 134

Chapter 10. Travel Tips & Practical Information — **139**
   10.1 Language, Currency & Tipping — 139
   10.2 Safety & Emergency Contacts — 143
   10.3 Budgeting & Connectivity — 147

Chapter 1. Introduction to Québec City

1.1 Overview of the City

Perched majestically along the banks of the St. Lawrence River in eastern Canada, Québec City is a destination unlike any other in North America. With its cobbled streets, towering stone fortifications, and the unmistakable spires of the Château Frontenac rising against the skyline, the city invites visitors into a realm where European elegance meets French-Canadian warmth. This is not just a place of beautiful sights, but one rich with culture, history, and identity.

Québec City is the capital of the province of Québec and is one of the oldest European settlements on the continent. Founded in **1608 by Samuel de Champlain**, it stands as the birthplace of French civilization in the Americas. Unlike many modern metropolises, Québec City has retained its old-world charm with remarkable authenticity, thanks in part to the preservation of its historic district — **Old Québec (Vieux-Québec)** — a UNESCO World Heritage Site.

What makes Québec City truly captivating is its blend of contrasts. Here, centuries-old ramparts and fortified walls cradle a lively modern city. French is the dominant language, yet the city pulses with international influences. Its winters are brisk and white, yet beautifully festive; its summers are vibrant and alive with festivals, terrace cafés, and riverside strolls.

The heart of the city is compact and walkable, making it ideal for slow exploration. Meander through the steep alleyways of **Petit Champlain**, sip warm cider in a cozy bistro during the winter carnival, or take in sweeping views of the Laurentian Mountains from the **Plains of Abraham**. Whether you're drawn by its history, cuisine, festivals, or simply the storybook atmosphere, Québec City offers a depth of experience that is both romantic and enriching.

Beyond the charm of the old town, Québec City boasts an artistic spirit and a passion for culture. Museums, galleries, and public performances are integral to daily life. The city has also become known for its culinary scene — a delicious blend of traditional Québécois comfort food and contemporary gastronomy, often made with local and seasonal ingredients.

Québec City is also a gateway to adventures beyond its walls. From the pastoral beauty of **Île d'Orléans** to the crashing waters of **Montmorency Falls**, and the cultural richness of **Wendake**, visitors can find a wealth of day trips just minutes from the city center.

Though it receives millions of visitors each year, Québec City maintains the feel of a small, welcoming town. Locals are proud of their heritage and traditions, and while French is the primary language, many are happy to engage with visitors in English and share the pride they hold for their home.

In all seasons and in every corner, Québec City tells a story — of its colonial past, of its enduring French roots, and of a people who have shaped a unique and vibrant identity. For travelers seeking history, beauty, culture, and heartfelt connection, Québec City is not merely a place to visit, but a place to remember.

1.2 Why Visit Québec City in 2025–2026

Visiting Québec City in 2025–2026 is an invitation to step into a living storybook — one where every season brings a new charm, and every street corner whispers tales of a rich past and a vibrant present. This historic city, steeped in French heritage and wrapped in

Old World elegance, is one of the most atmospheric and authentically European destinations in North America. And in the coming years, it offers even more reason to explore.

A Renaissance in Tourism & Culture

In recent years, Québec City has undergone a quiet but meaningful renaissance. Urban renewal projects, expanded cultural programming, new museum exhibits, and revitalized public spaces have transformed the visitor experience without compromising the city's historical soul. From new pedestrian zones in Old Québec to upgraded visitor centers and a fresh lineup of art festivals and performances, 2025–2026 promises to be an exciting period of both tradition and innovation.

The city's tourism board and local communities are working hand-in-hand to create sustainable tourism practices that not only preserve Québec's heritage but also offer more immersive, people-focused experiences. Travelers can now engage more deeply with the region's Indigenous cultures, participate in local culinary tours, and enjoy low-impact activities like riverfront cycling, historic walking trails, and community-led craft markets.

Year-Round Attractions & Events

Québec City has long been known as a four-season destination, and 2025–2026 will continue to showcase its diverse beauty throughout the year:

- **Winter 2025–2026**: Expect the **Carnaval de Québec** to return in full grandeur with ice sculptures, night parades, snow baths, and traditional music. New events are expected to enhance the experience, including international snow art competitions and expanded family-friendly activities.

- **Spring & Summer 2026**: The city blooms with outdoor concerts, sidewalk cafés, and vibrant energy. The **Festival d'été de Québec**, one of Canada's largest music festivals, draws artists and fans from around the world. The **New France Festival** in August celebrates the city's colonial roots with period costumes, reenactments, and immersive historic storytelling.

- **Autumn 2025**: Québec's fall foliage is breathtaking, with the city and its surroundings turning into a canvas of crimson, gold, and amber. It's the perfect season for gourmet food tours, wine tastings on Île d'Orléans, and cozy nights in charming inns.

A Unique Cultural Identity

Québec City is not just French-speaking — it's the beating heart of French-Canadian culture. From street names and architecture to cuisine and customs, the city's Francophone identity is alive and vibrant. But it's not closed off — it's welcoming. Visitors are embraced with a warm **"bonjour!"**, and there's a genuine pride in sharing Québec's rich heritage with others.

At a time when travelers seek destinations with depth and authenticity, Québec City stands out. It doesn't try to mimic elsewhere; it thrives on being exactly what it is — historical, romantic, creative, and proud.

Accessibility & Safety

Québec City continues to be one of the safest and most accessible cities for travelers in North America. Whether arriving by air, train, or cruise ship, the city's compact layout means attractions, accommodations, and dining are within close reach. Improved accessibility features in 2025–2026, including more wheelchair-friendly public spaces and upgraded signage, will ensure even more inclusive travel experiences.

Sustainable & Responsible Travel

As global awareness around responsible tourism grows, Québec City has emerged as a leader in green travel. The city supports eco-friendly hotels, low-emission public transport, extensive bike paths, and community-driven tourism. It's easy for visitors to enjoy the city while leaving a light footprint — whether by staying in LEED-certified accommodations, enjoying locally sourced menus, or choosing low-impact tours and activities.

Special Opportunities in 2025–2026

Several new and expanded attractions are planned during this travel period, including:

- The grand reopening of **Musée Royal 22e Régiment**, with interactive exhibits honoring Canada's military history.
- A redesigned **Montmorency Falls Visitor Center**, with improved hiking access and new viewing platforms.
- **Cultural programming in Wendake**, offering deeper insight into Huron-Wendat traditions, crafts, and cuisine.

For travelers seeking an unforgettable blend of old-world charm and 21st-century vitality, Québec City in 2025–2026 is a destination in its golden age. Whether you're planning your first visit or returning for more, there's always something fresh to discover behind the city's stone walls and winding alleys — a blend of the timeless and the new, waiting to be explored.

1.3 Brief History & Cultural Significance

Québec City's story begins on the rocky promontory of Cap Diamant, overlooking the St. Lawrence River — a location that would become the cradle of French civilization in North America. It was here, in **1608**, that **Samuel de Champlain**, a French explorer and cartographer, founded a permanent trading post that would evolve into one of the oldest European settlements on the continent. From this moment forward, Québec City became the epicenter of a cultural and geopolitical struggle that would shape the identity of Canada for centuries to come.

Colonial Foundations and the French Era

For more than 150 years, Québec thrived under French colonial rule. The settlement quickly grew into the capital of **New France**, serving as a critical hub for fur trading, missionary activity, and military strategy. Its natural fortifications — high cliffs and narrow passes — gave it strategic importance, while its architecture, modeled after French towns, reflected a desire to transplant European life to the New World.

Québec's early years were marked by encounters with Indigenous peoples, particularly the **Huron-Wendat Nation**, whose alliance and trade were essential to the colony's survival. These early exchanges laid the groundwork for both cooperation and conflict, elements that would recur throughout the city's colonial history.

Conquest and Transformation

A pivotal turning point came in **1759**, during the **Seven Years' War**. On the **Plains of Abraham**, just outside the city walls, British forces under General James Wolfe faced off against French troops led by General Louis-Joseph de Montcalm. In a battle that lasted barely an hour, both generals were mortally wounded, and the British claimed victory. This marked the fall of Québec to British control, and in **1763**, the Treaty of Paris formally ceded New France to Britain.

Despite the conquest, the French-speaking population remained the majority, and British authorities allowed many French laws, customs, and the **Catholic faith** to remain intact. This unusual coexistence led to a unique duality — a city ruled by Britain but deeply rooted in French identity. Over time, this dynamic evolved into a cultural resilience that still defines Québec City today.

The Capital of Francophone North America

Québec City would go on to play a foundational role in the creation of modern Canada. In 1867, when the provinces of Canada, New Brunswick, and Nova Scotia united under **Confederation**, Québec City emerged as the capital of the province of Québec. It remains so to this day, housing the **National Assembly** and the seat of provincial government.

While political power shifted and borders expanded, Québec City held fast to its **French linguistic and cultural heritage**. The city became a bastion of French-Canadian literature, music, and education, and its people led the charge in movements for language rights, cultural preservation, and provincial autonomy. Nowhere is this pride more visible than during Québec's many festivals, parades, and celebrations, which often blend religious, historical, and folk traditions.

Cultural Landmarks and Living Heritage

Québec City is the only walled city north of Mexico, and its **fortifications, gates, and cannons** are not simply relics — they are reminders of a city that has endured war, fire, revolution, and modern change. The historic district of **Old Québec** was recognized in **1985 as a UNESCO World Heritage Site**, a testament to its architectural integrity and significance in the story of colonization and cultural exchange.

The city's religious heritage is also profound, with **Notre-Dame de Québec Basilica-Cathedral** holding a place as the oldest church in Canada, and the only one outside Europe to have a Holy Door. Meanwhile, the **Citadel**, an active military installation, continues to anchor Québec's historic skyline, a living link to its defensive past.

Indigenous Roots and Reconnection

Before the arrival of Europeans, the region around Québec City was home to several Indigenous nations, including the **Wendat (Huron-Wendat)** people. Today, the nearby community of **Wendake** is a vital part of the city's cultural landscape, offering travelers an opportunity to learn about pre-colonial history, traditional knowledge, and ongoing Indigenous contributions to Québécois identity. As part of a broader movement of reconciliation and cultural revival, many local institutions are working to include Indigenous perspectives in museums, education, and tourism.

A City That Celebrates Its Identity

Québec City's cultural significance extends beyond its walls. It is often seen as the heart of **Francophone North America**, a place where the French language is not only preserved but passionately lived. Its role in fostering national pride, artistic innovation, and political dialogue has helped shape the identity of both Québec and Canada as a whole.

Every cobblestone in Old Québec, every song sung in its streets, every snowflake that falls during the winter carnival — they all carry the weight of a complex, layered, and fiercely proud heritage. This is not a city frozen in time, but one that remembers its past in order to build a vibrant future. Québec City's history is not merely a backdrop; it is a living, breathing force that defines its soul and charms all who wander through it.

Chapter 2. Getting to and Around Québec City

2.1 Arrival: Airports, Trains & Buses

Whether you're arriving from the globe or traveling from another part of Canada, Québec City is both accessible and welcoming. Its compact geography and well-developed transportation network make reaching the city seamless, whether you fly in, ride the rails, or arrive by bus.

Jean Lesage International Airport (YQB)

Main Gateway to the City

Located just 16 kilometers (10 miles) west of downtown, **Jean Lesage International Airport** (Aéroport international Jean-Lesage de Québec) is the primary airport serving the Québec City region. It's a modern, efficient terminal that handles over a million passengers annually and continues to expand its connections.

Key Features:

- **Domestic and International Flights**: Regular service from major Canadian cities (Montreal, Toronto, Ottawa, Halifax, Calgary), as well as seasonal or direct international flights from the U.S. (Newark, Chicago, Fort Lauderdale), Europe (Paris), Mexico, and the Caribbean.
- **Services**: Free Wi-Fi, cafés, car rental desks, taxi & shuttle services, currency exchange, and bilingual signage throughout.
- **Transportation to Downtown**:
    - **Taxi**: Approx. 20–30 minutes to downtown; flat rate around **CAD $40**.
    - **Public Bus (RTC Route 76)**: Connects the airport to the **Sainte-Foy** bus/train station and **Metrobus lines**, running every 30 minutes during peak times.
    - **Car Rental**: Available on-site with major providers including Avis, Budget, Enterprise, and Hertz.

Website: https://www.aeroportdequebec.com

Via Rail – Québec City Station (Gare du Palais)

Arrive by Train – Elegance in Motion

If you're seeking a scenic and relaxed way to arrive, **Via Rail Canada** offers comfortable and efficient train service directly into Québec City's historic **Gare du Palais**. This Beaux-Arts style station is a destination in itself — centrally located and beautifully preserved.

Key Routes & Times:

- **From Montreal**: Approx. **3.5 hours** via the Québec-Montreal corridor; frequent daily departures.
- **From Ottawa/Toronto**: Trains connect via Montreal.
- **From Halifax**: A longer journey via connections, ideal for those exploring the Maritimes.

Why Choose the Train?

- Spacious seating, scenic views of the St. Lawrence River and countryside, onboard Wi-Fi, and café services.
- Eco-friendly and ideal for slow travel lovers.

- Direct access to Old Québec and nearby hotels upon arrival.

Website: https://www.viarail.ca

Long-Distance & Intercity Bus Services

Affordable and Convenient

Québec City is well-served by reliable long-distance bus operators, offering affordable routes throughout Québec and neighboring provinces.

Gare du Palais Bus Terminal

Located within the same building as the train station, it serves as the main hub for intercity buses.

Top Operators:

- **Orléans Express**: Connects Québec City to **Montreal** (3–4 hours), **Trois-Rivières, Rimouski, Gaspé**, and other destinations across the province.
- **Intercar**: Provides service to **Saguenay, Lac-Saint-Jean, Charlevoix**, and **North Shore** regions.

Bus Travel Highlights:

- Affordable pricing (one-way to Montreal starts at approx. **CAD $35–$50**).
- Luggage storage, Wi-Fi on board (on most routes), and easy transfers.
- Great for budget travelers or those preferring not to drive.

Websites:
https://www.orleansexpress.com
https://www.intercar.ca

Cruise Port (Port de Québec)

Arrival by Water – A Grand Entrance

Québec City is a popular stop for **St. Lawrence River cruises**, with the **Port of Québec** welcoming over 100 cruise ships annually between May and October. Passengers disembark right at the foot of Old Québec, within walking distance of iconic landmarks.

Services:

- Visitor information center right at the terminal
- Taxis, shuttles, and walking access into the historic district
- Luggage handling, rest areas, and local guides for excursions

Perfect for: River cruise travelers, European-style voyages, or anyone exploring eastern Canada's waterways.

Website: https://www.portquebec.ca

Driving into Québec City

Those coming from **Montreal, Ottawa, or Eastern U.S. states** may prefer to drive. Highways are well-maintained year-round, with scenic routes along the **Trans-Canada Highway (Autoroute 20/40)** and **Autoroute 73** providing smooth entry into the city.

- **Montreal to Québec City**: Approx. **2.5 to 3 hours**
- **Ottawa**: Around **5 hours**
- **Boston**: About **6.5 hours**
- **Parking**: Available throughout the city, with many garages and hotels offering overnight options. Rates vary from CAD $15–$25/day.

Final Arrival Tips:

- **Peak Travel Periods**: Summer (June–August), Winter Carnival (late Jan–early Feb), and fall foliage (Sept–Oct).
- **Language Note**: French is the primary language; most transport signage and staff are bilingual.
- **Currency**: Canadian Dollar (CAD); credit/debit cards widely accepted.

With multiple accessible travel options — by air, rail, road, or river — arriving in Québec City is not only easy but often scenic and memorable. Whether you're stepping off a plane, rolling in by train, or sailing into the historic port, the city's timeless charm welcomes you the moment you arrive.

2.2 Public Transport, Taxis & Ride-Sharing

Once you've arrived in Québec City, getting around is both convenient and enjoyable. Despite its historic roots and cobblestone streets, the city boasts a modern and efficient transportation network, particularly suited for travelers who prefer not to rent a car.

From reliable public buses to friendly local taxis and modern ride-hailing services, Québec City offers several smart options to explore the city with ease.

Réseau de Transport de la Capitale (RTC) – Québec City's Public Bus System

The city's primary public transportation provider, **RTC (Réseau de transport de la Capitale)**, operates a well-connected, safe, and punctual bus system that services the greater Québec City area. It's the most cost-effective way to get around, especially for those staying multiple days or exploring beyond the core districts.

Key Routes for Visitors:

- **Métrobus 800/801**: High-frequency lines that serve major tourist zones, including Old Québec, Montcalm, Parliament Hill, and Sainte-Foy.
- **Route 11**: Scenic route connecting Old Québec with Montmorency Falls, the Museum of Civilization, and the Petit Champlain district.
- **Route 1**: Loops around the Upper and Lower Towns, ideal for short hops through historic areas.

Fares & Passes (2025 Rates):

- **Single fare**: CAD $3.75 (valid for 90 minutes, transfers included)
- **1-Day Pass**: CAD $9.25 (unlimited travel for 24 hours)
- **Weekend Pass**: CAD $18.50 (valid Friday evening through Sunday)
- **Children (under 6)** ride free with a paying adult

Where to Buy Tickets:

- Onboard (exact change required)
- RTC Espace kiosks, convenience stores (dépanneurs), and select hotels
- Mobile via **RTC Nomade Payment App** (tap-and-pay option)

Traveler Tips:

- Buses run from **5:30 a.m. to midnight** (some night lines available)
- Download the **RTC Nomade app** for real-time bus schedules, maps, and fare purchases
- Buses are bilingual, and digital signage displays stops clearly

Website: https://www.rtcquebec.ca

Taxi Services

Taxis are widely available throughout Québec City, especially in central areas, hotel zones, and near major attractions. They are safe, regulated, and operated by courteous bilingual drivers.

Major Taxi Companies:

- **Taxi Coop Québec** – Tel: +1 418-525-5191
- **Taxi Laurier** – Tel: +1 418-651-2727
- **Taxi Québec** – Tel: +1 418-522-2001

Rates (2025 Estimate):

- Base fare: CAD $4.20
- Per kilometer: CAD $1.90
- Airport to downtown (fixed rate): Approx. **CAD $40–$45**

Taxis can be hailed on the street, booked by phone, or reserved through the company's mobile apps. Many vehicles accept credit/debit cards, but it's always good to confirm when entering.

When to Use Taxis:

- Late-night travel when buses are less frequent
- Quick transfers between districts or during inclement weather
- Traveling with luggage or groups

Ride-Sharing & Mobile Hailing

Québec City has embraced ride-hailing, offering visitors the comfort and convenience of app-based transportation.

Available Services:

- **Uber** – Widely used across the city, especially popular with younger travelers and those familiar with the app.
- **Eva** – A local cooperative ride-sharing platform based in Québec, offering ethical pricing and support for local drivers. Available in French and English.

Both platforms allow for real-time fare estimates, cashless payment, and options for shared or premium rides. Pick-up locations are clearly marked around major transport hubs like Gare du Palais and Jean Lesage Airport.

Pros of Ride-Sharing:

- Transparent pricing and estimated arrival times
- No need to carry cash
- Flexible options (UberX, Comfort, Pool, etc.)

Public Transport vs. Private Rides – What's Best for You?

Travel Option	Best For	Price Range	Notes
RTC Buses	Budget travelers, eco-conscious explorers	Low (CAD $3.75–$9.25)	Frequent service, especially downtown
Taxis	Convenience, fast local travel	Medium to High	Always available, especially at night
Ride-Sharing	App-savvy visitors, group travel	Moderate	Seamless booking and route tracking

Accessible Travel

RTC buses and most taxi services accommodate passengers with mobility needs. **All Métrobus vehicles** are low-floor and wheelchair accessible. If you require accessible taxis, it's best to request them in advance when booking through local dispatch services.

Final Transport Tips for Visitors:

- Rush hour in Québec City is typically **7:00–9:00 a.m.** and **4:00–6:00 p.m.** Plan travel accordingly.
- While Old Québec is very walkable, bus and ride options are essential for exploring suburbs or reaching outlying attractions like **Montmorency Falls** or **Wendake**.
- Most drivers speak both **French and English**, especially in tourism-heavy areas, so communication is rarely an issue.

With a strong public transport network, trusted taxi services, and modern ride-sharing apps, getting around Québec City is not only simple — it's part of the travel experience itself. Whether you're hopping on a city bus to see the Château Frontenac at sunrise, or gliding through the streets with a ride-hailing app after dinner, the city offers flexible options that cater to every kind of traveler.

2.3 Renting a Car or Bike

While Québec City is delightfully compact and walkable, especially in and around Old Québec, some travelers prefer the freedom and flexibility of renting a car or a bicycle—especially if they plan to explore beyond the city walls. Whether you're venturing to the pastoral beauty of **Île d'Orléans**, heading out to **Montmorency Falls**, or simply prefer to move at your own pace, car and bike rentals offer excellent options for independent travel.

Renting a Car

Car rental is ideal for visitors planning day trips or overnight getaways outside Québec City. Though not necessary for city-center exploration, it becomes invaluable for rural drives, wine routes, or visiting remote sites like **Le Massif de Charlevoix** or the **Jacques-Cartier National Park**.

Major Car Rental Companies:

Car rental agencies are conveniently located at both **Jean Lesage International Airport** and in downtown areas near **Gare du Palais** and **Place d'Youville**.

- **Enterprise Rent-A-Car** – www.enterprise.ca
- **Hertz** – www.hertz.ca
- **Budget** – www.budget.ca
- **Avis** – www.avis.ca
- **Discount Québec** – Local provider with good rates and flexible terms

Rental Information (2025 Rates):

- **Daily Rental**: Approx. **CAD $55–$90** (compact to mid-size vehicles)
- **Age Requirement**: Minimum **21 years old** (some agencies charge a young driver fee for under 25)
- **Driver's License**: Valid license from your home country; International Driving Permit recommended for non-French documents
- **Insurance**: Basic coverage included; extended coverage available at extra cost
- **Fuel**: Most rentals operate on a **"full-to-full"** fuel policy

Parking Considerations:

- Paid street parking and garages available downtown; rates range from **CAD $2.50 to $4.00/hour**
- Many hotels offer guest parking for **CAD $15–$25/day**
- Avoid driving in Old Québec's Upper Town during peak times—narrow streets and limited spots

Best Use Cases:

- Day trips to **Île d'Orléans**, **Wendake**, or **Baie-Saint-Paul**
- Exploring wine and cider routes
- Outdoor activities in regional parks and winter ski trips

Renting a Bike

Cycling is one of the best ways to discover Québec City and its stunning riverfront landscapes. The city has invested heavily in its cycling infrastructure, offering over **400 km of bike paths**, scenic greenways, and dedicated lanes.

Whether you're coasting along the **Samuel-De Champlain Promenade**, pedaling across the **Pierre-Laporte Bridge** toward Lévis, or venturing up to Montmorency Falls on the **Corridor du Littoral**, there are routes suited for every level of rider.

Bike Rental Shops:

- **Cyclo Services**
  289 Rue Saint-Paul, Vieux-Port
  City bikes, electric bikes, tandems, and guided tours
  Rates: From **CAD $25 for 2 hours**, full day approx. **CAD $45**
  www.cycloservices.net

- **Tuque & Bicycle Expériences**
  835 Avenue de Vimy, near Old Québec
  Rentals, maintenance, and curated cycling experiences
  E-bikes from **CAD $50/day**, hybrid bikes from **CAD $35/day**
  www.tuqueetbicycle.com

- **Location Echo Sports**
  50 Rue du Marché-Champlain
  City and trail bikes, accessories, child trailers
  Affordable hourly and day rates
  www.echosports.ca

Popular Cycling Routes:

- **Corridor du Littoral**: A stunning 50 km path along the St. Lawrence River, from Old Port to Montmorency Falls and Beauport.
- **Promenade Samuel-De Champlain**: A newly redeveloped 6 km waterside path with panoramic views, public art, and green spaces.
- **Plains of Abraham Loop**: Ride through the city's most historic park with sweeping river views and shaded lawns.
- **Ferry to Lévis**: Combine your ride with a quick crossing (15 minutes) to explore the picturesque bike trails of Lévis.

Tips for Cyclists:

- Helmets are not mandatory for adults but are strongly recommended and usually provided.
- Many paths are shared with pedestrians—ring your bell and ride respectfully.
- Late spring to early autumn is the best time for cycling; winter bike rentals are limited.

Bike-Sharing (Québec sur 2 Roues – Coming 2025)

In 2025, Québec City is expected to launch a **public bike-sharing system**, offering short-term rentals through automated kiosks around town. The program, similar to Montréal's BIXI, will allow easy, spontaneous rides for tourists and locals alike. Look out for updates at tourist information centers and the RTC website.

Which Option Is Right for You?

Transportation Type	Best For	Pros	Considerations
Car Rental	Day trips, regional excursions, family travel	Total independence, access to remote areas	Downtown traffic, parking fees
Bike Rental	Active travelers, scenic explorers	Eco-friendly, scenic routes, affordable	Terrain can be hilly in parts of the city
E-Bikes	Long rides or hilly terrain	Effortless climbing, fast travel	Higher rental cost

Final Tips:

- For city-only visits, bikes are more efficient and environmentally friendly.
- If you're visiting in **autumn**, car rentals are perfect for exploring fall colors in the countryside.
- Combine both: Rent a bike for local discoveries and a car for day trips beyond the city.

Whether you're gliding past historic battlements on two wheels or winding through country roads in a rental car, Québec City offers flexible transportation options to match every travel style. The journey — as much as the destination — is part of the magic.

Chapter 3: Top Attractions in Québec City

3.1 Old Québec (Vieux-Québec) – UNESCO Site

A Brief Story

Old Québec, or *Vieux-Québec*, is more than a historic district; it is the birthplace of French civilization in North America and a cornerstone of Canadian identity. Established in 1608 by Samuel de Champlain, this area became the capital of New France and played a pivotal role in the continent's colonial history. With its formidable cliffside location overlooking the St. Lawrence River, it served as both a strategic military stronghold and a center of trade, culture, and religion. Over the centuries, it has weathered wars, sieges, political shifts, and social transformation. Today, it remains the only walled city north of Mexico and one of the best-preserved examples of a fortified colonial settlement in the Western Hemisphere.

In 1985, UNESCO recognized its outstanding universal value and designated Old Québec as a World Heritage Site. Its ramparts, gates, historic buildings, and charming streets bear witness to over four centuries of history and the continuous interaction between the French and British colonial empires, Indigenous peoples, and modern Canadian society.

Location

Old Québec occupies the historic core of Québec City, bordered by Rue Saint-Jean, Avenue Honoré-Mercier, Rue des Remparts, and the St. Lawrence River. It consists of two principal areas:

- **Haute-Ville (Upper Town)**: Located on Cap Diamant, this area is home to key landmarks such as Château Frontenac, the Citadelle, and the city's primary religious and governmental buildings.
- **Basse-Ville (Lower Town)**: Nestled at the base of the cliffs along the river, this area includes the Quartier Petit Champlain, Place Royale, and the Old Port.

Admission Price

There is no fee to enter or explore Old Québec itself. The district is a public area, freely accessible at all times. However, some individual attractions within Old Québec—such as museums, the Citadel, or guided walking tours—may charge admission fees ranging from CAD 5 to CAD 25.

Website & Contact Information

- Official Tourism Portal: https://www.quebec-cite.com/en/old-quebec
- Phone: +1 877-783-1608 (Tourisme Québec)

Opening Hours

Old Québec is accessible year-round, 24 hours a day. Most shops, museums, restaurants, and services operate from approximately 9:00 AM to 6:00 PM, though many stay open later during the summer months and holidays. Public transportation and walking access are always available, and the area is safe to visit day or night.

Key Features

1. Fortified Walls and Gates: The city's original defenses include over 4.6 kilometers of walls and four main gates: Porte Saint-Jean, Porte Saint-Louis, Porte Prescott, and Porte Kent. These offer panoramic views, interpretive panels, and direct access to the historic city center.

2. Château Frontenac: Perched high on the promontory, this grand hotel, built in 1893, is a symbol of the city. Though a luxury accommodation, the hotel is open to the public and offers guided historical tours.

3. Terrasse Dufferin: A wooden boardwalk extending along the cliff's edge in front of Château Frontenac, offering sweeping views of the St. Lawrence River and access to archaeological remains of Champlain's original habitation.

4. The Citadel of Québec: A star-shaped fortress still used by the Canadian military. It includes the Royal 22e Régiment Museum and hosts the Changing of the Guard ceremony in summer.

5. Place Royale: The original town square where Champlain founded Québec. It's now surrounded by 17th- and 18th-century buildings and anchored by Notre-Dame-des-Victoires Church.

6. Quartier Petit Champlain: A pedestrian-only shopping district full of narrow lanes, artisan boutiques, bistros, and seasonal decorations.

7. Fresque des Québécois: A massive trompe-l'œil mural that blends historical and modern figures, illustrating the story of Québec.

8. Religious Architecture: Including the Notre-Dame de Québec Basilica-Cathedral, which houses a Holy Door, and the Ursuline Monastery, both of which reflect the deep spiritual roots of the city.

9. Streetscapes and Architecture: Cobblestone lanes, mansard roofs, wrought-iron balconies, and traditional stone houses reflect French, British, and North American architectural styles spanning three centuries.

Visitor Services

- **Tourist Information Centers**: Located near Château Frontenac and Place d'Armes, offering maps, brochures, and multilingual assistance.
- **Public Washrooms**: Available at major plazas including Place Royale and Place d'Armes.
- **Interpretive Signage**: Bilingual (French and English) historical plaques and QR codes provide contextual information.
- **Transportation Links**: Old Québec is serviced by the RTC (local bus network), pedestrian paths, and a funicular connecting Upper and Lower Town.
- **Guided Tours**: Available daily, including historical walking tours, ghost tours, food tours, and heritage-focused experiences.

- **Accessibility**: While Old Québec's cobbled terrain poses some mobility challenges, many areas have been retrofitted with ramps and adapted facilities. The funicular is wheelchair-accessible.
- **Dining and Shopping**: The area features a mix of traditional bakeries, gourmet restaurants, craft stores, and souvenir shops.
- **Seasonal Events**: Hosts major events such as Carnaval de Québec, Fête de la Nouvelle-France, summer street performance festivals, and the German Christmas Market.

Description

Old Québec exudes atmosphere. Its layered identity is felt in every corner—a living blend of French colonial elegance, British regimental order, and Canadian resilience. Divided into the Upper and Lower Towns, each section provides a unique lens through which to view the city.

In **Upper Town**, the skyline is dominated by Château Frontenac, with its fairytale turrets and copper roof. Visitors wander through Place d'Armes and along Rue Saint-Louis, past governmental buildings like the Parliament and iconic religious sites such as the Notre-Dame Basilica. The **Fortifications of Québec National Historic Site** offers a self-guided walk atop the walls, punctuated by cannons and interpretive posts. The area is quieter in the early morning and glows golden under the late afternoon sun.

In **Lower Town**, accessed via the Breakneck Stairs or the Funicular, visitors step back into the intimate charm of New France. The Quartier Petit Champlain feels like an open-air museum: flower boxes spill over stone windowsills, fairy lights twinkle year-round, and buskers fill the air with music. Place Royale, where Champlain laid the city's first stones, remains an architectural jewel.

Unlike other historic quarters that feel frozen in time, Old Québec is vibrantly lived in. Locals sip coffee at sidewalk cafés, children play in pocket parks, and artisans create and sell their wares just as they have for generations. The blending of past and present is seamless and soulful.

This district is best explored slowly. Walk with intention, allow time for discovery, and don't hesitate to veer off the main paths. Some of the most rewarding experiences come from serendipitous encounters: a hidden courtyard, a centuries-old fresco, or a musician playing a chanson in the twilight.

Old Québec is not merely a place to see but a place to feel. It is a narrative etched into stone, told in French and English, whispered through alleyways, and celebrated by all who wander its timeless streets.

3.2 Château Frontenac

A Brief Story

Perched atop Cap Diamant, gazing out over the St. Lawrence River, the Château Frontenac is more than just a hotel—it is the crown jewel of Québec City and one of the most iconic buildings in Canada. Commissioned by the Canadian Pacific Railway and opened in 1893, it was part of a grand vision to promote luxury tourism across Canada. Its architect, Bruce Price, designed the hotel in the dramatic Châteauesque style, drawing inspiration from French Renaissance castles. With its steep copper roofs, ornate turrets, and grand silhouette, it instantly became a symbol of elegance and prosperity.

Named after Louis de Buade, Comte de Frontenac, the governor of New France in the late 1600s, the hotel has witnessed over a century of history. It hosted Winston Churchill and Franklin D. Roosevelt during the pivotal Québec Conferences of World War II, where Allied leaders planned the invasion of Normandy. Over the decades, it has welcomed royalty, heads of state, celebrities, and countless travelers from across the globe.

More than a hotel, the Château Frontenac is an enduring cultural landmark. It has become synonymous with Québec City itself—its proud silhouette etched into the skyline, its history intertwined with the city's soul.

Location

Château Frontenac is located in the heart of Old Québec's Upper Town:

- **Address**: 1 Rue des Carrières, Québec City, QC G1R 4P5, Canada
- **Overlooks**: Terrasse Dufferin and the St. Lawrence River
- **Proximity**: Adjacent to Place d'Armes and a short walk from the Citadelle, Notre-Dame Basilica, and the Funicular to Lower Town

Admission Price

While the hotel itself is not an attraction with a general admission fee, there are guided tours available for non-guests:

- **Guided Historical Tour**: CAD 20–30 per person
- **Access to public areas (lobby, boutiques, and restaurants)**: Free
- Hotel guests enjoy additional access to lounges, spa facilities, and exclusive viewing areas

Website & Contact Information

- **Website**: https://www.fairmont.com/frontenac-quebec/
- **Phone**: +1 418-692-3861

Opening Hours

- **Hotel Lobby and Boutique Areas**: Open daily, 7:00 AM to 11:00 PM
- **Guided Tours**: Multiple daily tours available; reservations recommended
- **Restaurants and Cafés**: Vary by venue, typically open 7:00 AM to 10:00 PM
- **Hotel Services**: 24/7 for registered guests

Key Features

1. Historic Architecture: The hotel's design reflects the romanticism of European castles, with steep pitched roofs, corner towers, and elaborate detailing in stone and copper.

2. Grande Allée Lobby: A majestic, richly decorated interior with period furnishings, chandeliers, and historical exhibits.

3. Guided Tours: Explore areas not typically accessible to the public, including rooms where historic meetings were held.

4. Restaurants:

- *Le Champlain*: Fine French cuisine in a regal setting
- *1608 Wine & Cheese Bar*: Specializing in local pairings with river views
- *Place Dufferin*: Breakfast and brunch with panoramic windows

5. Boutique Shops: Upscale Canadian and Québécois-made items, artisanal chocolates, and hotel-branded merchandise

6. Events & Weddings: Lavish ballrooms and salons make it a popular venue for upscale events

7. Spa & Wellness Center: Includes massage therapy, fitness room, and indoor pool

8. Terrace and River Views: Many areas of the hotel offer sweeping vistas of the St. Lawrence River, Île d'Orléans, and Lévis

9. Historic Rooms: Themed suites inspired by famous guests and events

Visitor Services

- **Multilingual Staff**: English and French are spoken throughout
- **Accessibility**: Fully accessible entrances and elevators
- **Wi-Fi Access**: Complimentary for guests, available in lobby for visitors
- **Public Restrooms**: Available near the main lobby
- **On-Site Parking**: Valet and self-parking options for a fee
- **Concierge Services**: Provides information, bookings, and recommendations
- **Children and Pet Friendly**: Services and amenities available for families

Description

The Château Frontenac dominates the skyline of Québec City like a fairy-tale fortress. From nearly every corner of the Old City, its copper roof and commanding towers can be seen rising above the rooftops, drawing travelers toward its storied walls. While its appearance is palatial, what lies within is equally compelling.

Stepping into the grand lobby, visitors are greeted by a blend of Edwardian elegance and Québécois warmth. Wood-paneled walls, grand staircases, stained glass, and velvet armchairs evoke the glamour of the early 20th century. Throughout the public spaces, curated exhibits and photographs recount the hotel's illustrious past. It was here that the leaders of the Allied powers met during the Second World War, and where dignitaries toasted the future over fine wine and local cheese.

The hotel's rooms and suites vary from classically styled chambers with antique touches to sleek modern suites equipped with luxury amenities. Many rooms offer views that sweep across the St. Lawrence, especially magical at sunrise or after dusk when the river lights begin to sparkle.

Dining at the Château is an experience in itself. *Le Champlain* serves elegant multi-course meals that pay tribute to French culinary tradition, often with seasonal Québécois ingredients. Meanwhile, the *1608 Wine & Cheese Bar* provides an intimate space for sampling regional pairings, with sommeliers on hand to guide you.

Outside, the hotel opens onto **Terrasse Dufferin**, a public boardwalk where musicians perform, artists paint, and couples stroll. Beneath the terrace lie the archaeological remains of Champlain's habitation, accessible through the **Saint-Louis Forts and Châteaux National Historic Site**.

What makes Château Frontenac more than just a place to stay or visit is its role in shaping the narrative of Québec. It is not only a symbol of luxury and heritage but also a living monument to diplomacy, art, and community. Locals celebrate it with pride, and for many, it is the site of cherished memories: engagements, weddings, and anniversaries.

For visitors, a walk through its halls is a journey through Canadian history and French elegance. Whether sipping coffee under a vaulted ceiling, wandering the halls where Churchill walked, or admiring the glow of its façade during the winter carnival, the Château Frontenac offers a rich, immersive experience like no other.

A visit to Québec City is not complete without spending time at the Château—whether for a few nights, a meal, or simply a quiet moment on its terrace. Here, history is not just preserved. It is lived, every day.

3.3 Montmorency Falls Park (Parc de la Chute-Montmorency)

A Brief Story

Long before Jacques Cartier explored the region in the 16th century, Montmorency Falls was revered by the Indigenous peoples who lived near the banks of the St. Lawrence River. Later, when Samuel de Champlain founded Québec in 1608, the towering cascade became a prominent natural landmark visible to early settlers arriving by boat. The falls were named after Charles de Montmorency, an admiral and nobleman of the French court. In the centuries that followed, the site evolved from an untamed wilderness to a place of strategic and recreational significance. It played host to early industry, saw the construction of mills and hydroelectric installations, and was eventually preserved and developed into one of Québec's most spectacular public parks.

Today, Montmorency Falls Park stands as a remarkable example of how natural beauty and human accessibility can coexist. At 83 meters tall, the falls are nearly 30 meters higher than Niagara Falls, making them among the tallest in the province. Whether frozen in dramatic cascades in winter or thundering with snowmelt in spring, the falls captivate visitors with their sheer power and elegance.

Location

- **Address**: 5300 Boulevard Sainte-Anne, Québec City, QC G1C 1S1, Canada
- **Proximity**: Approximately 12 kilometers (15 minutes) east of Old Québec
- **Coordinates**: 46.8904° N, 71.1503° W

Montmorency Falls Park is located at the mouth of the Montmorency River, where it plunges off a cliff into the St. Lawrence River, just before the bridge to Île d'Orléans.

Admission Price

- **General Admission**: CAD 7.39 per adult (tax included)
- **Children under 17**: Free with an adult
- **Gondola Ride**: CAD 15.70 round trip
- **Via Ferrata Experience**: Starting at CAD 41.75
- **Zipline (seasonal)**: From CAD 35 per person
- **Annual Pass**: Available for frequent visitors

Website & Contact Information

- **Website**: https://www.sepaq.com/pq/mch
- **Phone**: +1 418-663-3330

Opening Hours

- **Park Grounds**: Open daily, year-round, 9:00 AM to 5:00 PM (longer in summer)
- **Visitor Center & Boutique**: 9:00 AM to 6:00 PM (seasonal hours apply)
- **Gondola & Zipline**: Open seasonally from late May through early October

Key Features

1. Montmorency Falls: The centerpiece of the park, the waterfall cascades over a cliff of ancient rock, offering an awe-inspiring display of natural power. Best viewed from multiple angles for full appreciation.

2. Suspension Bridge: Spanning the crest of the falls, this bridge offers dizzying views down into the plunge pool below and panoramic views across the river.

3. Cable Car (Gondola): A scenic ride that carries visitors from the base of the falls to the clifftop, providing effortless access to the suspension bridge and upper trails.

4. Panoramic Staircase: A series of 487 steps climbing up the cliffside, allowing energetic visitors to hike beside the falls and stop at viewing platforms along the way.

5. Manoir Montmorency: A historic mansion near the top of the falls, home to a restaurant, exhibition space, boutique, and reception halls.

6. Via Ferrata: A guided climbing experience with fixed cables and ladders built into the cliff, offering adrenaline-pumping views.

7. Zipline: For the adventurous, the zipline offers an exhilarating ride across the face of the falls.

8. Ice Climbing (Winter): One of the rare places in Canada where visitors can ice climb a frozen waterfall under expert supervision.

Visitor Services

- **Visitor Center**: Offers maps, trail guides, and multilingual staff
- **Boutique & Souvenirs**: Located in Manoir Montmorency
- **Restaurant & Café**: Local cuisine with stunning views of the river and falls
- **Restrooms**: Available throughout the park
- **Parking**: Paid parking available at both base and summit access points
- **Picnic Areas**: Designated spots with tables and shade for family-friendly outings
- **Guided Tours**: Available on request, including nature walks and historical insights
- **Accessibility**: Gondola, suspension bridge, and upper viewing areas are wheelchair accessible

Description

Montmorency Falls Park is a place where nature takes center stage but is thoughtfully complemented by well-designed facilities that allow visitors of all ages and fitness levels to engage with the environment. From the moment one enters the park, the sound of crashing water and the scent of mist fill the air. In warmer months, wildflowers bloom along trails and the falls thunder with snowmelt. In winter, the entire scene transforms into a crystalline cathedral of ice.

Visitors typically begin at the **base of the falls**, where a broad platform offers direct views of the torrent as it hits the basin below. The sheer verticality and constant roar of the water provide a visceral sense of nature's strength. From here, visitors can choose to hike the panoramic staircase, board the cable car, or linger by the riverside for photos.

At the **top of the cliff**, the **suspension bridge** offers a heart-pounding perspective as it sways slightly above the chasm. From this vantage point, one can see not just the crest of the falls, but also the expanse of the St. Lawrence River, the bridges to Île d'Orléans, and even the towers of downtown Québec City in the distance.

Near the suspension bridge sits the **Manoir Montmorency**, a stately building that has hosted governors and dignitaries for over two centuries. Today, it functions as a hospitality center where visitors can enjoy regional dishes in the dining room or explore temporary exhibits on the region's geology and history.

For thrill-seekers, the **Via Ferrata** offers a cliffside adventure with safety harnesses and expert guides, while the **zipline** allows guests to soar directly above the falls—an unforgettable rush.

In winter, the falls freeze into a dramatic wall of ice. Adventurous climbers ascend with crampons and axes, while spectators marvel at the natural sculptures and snow-covered trails. Ice climbing lessons and rentals are available through park services.

Families will appreciate the **well-marked trails**, safe viewing platforms, and kid-friendly learning zones. Photographers will find endless compositions: rainbows in the mist, moonlit cascades, and golden-hour reflections.

Montmorency Falls Park serves as a natural amphitheater of sensory experiences. Every season reveals a different aspect of its beauty, from spring torrents and summer greenery to autumn foliage and winter frost. It is both a destination for peaceful reflection and high-energy adventure.

Accessible, awe-inspiring, and deeply rooted in the region's history, Montmorency Falls Park is more than a sightseeing stop—it is an immersive natural wonder that remains etched in memory long after the visit ends.

3.4 Plains of Abraham & The Citadel

A Brief Story

The **Plains of Abraham** and **The Citadel** represent the historical heartbeat of Québec City, where the past unfolds across rolling green fields and star-shaped fortifications. In 1759, during the Seven Years' War, these plains were the dramatic site of a pivotal battle between British General James Wolfe and French General Louis-Joseph de Montcalm. Within a mere 15 minutes, the British secured a decisive victory, altering the fate of New France and paving the way for British dominance in Canada.

Today, the area remains a powerful symbol of Canadian identity and resilience, and forms part of **Battlefields Park**, one of the oldest and most significant urban parks in the country. The Citadel ("La Citadelle de Québec"), situated on Cap Diamant above the plains, complements the site with its formidable walls, ceremonial traditions, and status as an active military installation. Together, these landmarks bridge past and present—a confluence of history, national pride, and cultural preservation.

Location

- **Plains of Abraham**: Avenue Wilfrid-Laurier, Québec City, QC G1R 2L3, Canada
- **The Citadel**: 1 Côte de la Citadelle, Québec City, QC G1R 3R2, Canada
- **Proximity**: Both are located within walking distance of Old Québec, just beyond the fortified walls and adjacent to Parliament Hill

Admission Price

- **Plains of Abraham**: Free entry to park grounds and walking paths
- **Museum of the Plains of Abraham**:
    - Adults: CAD 5.65
    - Children under 12: Free
- **The Citadel** (Guided tour and museum included):
    - Adults: CAD 18
    - Children (7–11): CAD 6
    - Family rate available

Website & Contact Information

- **Plains of Abraham**: https://www.ccbn-nbc.gc.ca
- **The Citadel**: https://www.lacitadelle.qc.ca
- **Phone** (Battlefields Park): +1 418-648-4071
- **Phone** (The Citadel): +1 418-694-2815

Opening Hours

- **Plains of Abraham**: Open year-round, 5:00 AM to 11:00 PM
- **Museum of the Plains of Abraham**: Daily, 9:00 AM to 5:30 PM (hours may vary by season)
- **The Citadel**:
    - Summer: Daily, 9:00 AM to 5:00 PM
    - Winter: Closed on some holidays; hours may be reduced

Key Features

1. Plains of Abraham

- Expansive green space covering over 98 hectares
- Historic battlefield with interpretive panels and memorials
- Outdoor concerts, festivals, and sports fields

- Cross-country skiing and snowshoeing trails in winter

2. Museum of the Plains of Abraham

- Engaging exhibits on the 1759 battle and military history
- Multimedia presentations and educational programs
- Temporary art and history exhibits

3. The Citadel of Québec

- Star-shaped fortress built between 1820–1850
- Official residence of the Governor General of Canada (second home)
- Active base for the Royal 22e Régiment ("Van Doos")
- Military museum with exhibits on Canadian Armed Forces
- Scenic overlook offering stunning river views

4. Changing of the Guard

- Held daily during summer (late June to early September)
- Traditional ceremony performed by soldiers in full regalia
- Includes Batisse the goat, regimental mascot

5. Martello Towers

- 19th-century stone towers used for defense
- Accessible to visitors in summer, offering insights into military strategy

6. Joan of Arc Garden

- Formal garden featuring bronze statue and seasonal floral designs
- Peaceful place for rest, reading, or reflection

Visitor Services

- **Information Kiosks**: Located near the museum and main park entrances
- **Restrooms**: Available at the museum, Citadel, and select areas in the park
- **Guided Tours**: Bilingual tours offered at The Citadel and Battlefield Park
- **Picnic Areas**: Shaded spots with benches and tables
- **Bicycle Rentals**: Available seasonally near Grand Allée entrance
- **Accessibility**: Museum and key trails are wheelchair accessible
- **Winter Facilities**: Groomed trails and equipment rentals for snow sports
- **Public Art and Installations**: Found throughout the park

Description

The **Plains of Abraham** serve as the green lungs of Québec City—a sanctuary of peace shaped by the turbulence of history. When visitors walk its pathways today, they tread the very ground where the fate of New France was decided in the 18th century. Despite the site's military origins, it has become a place of culture, leisure, and remembrance.

During warmer months, the plains are alive with picnickers, joggers, and families enjoying the open lawns. Locals walk their dogs, children fly kites, and couples enjoy panoramic views from the cliffside paths. In summer, the site transforms into a venue for major festivals such as the Festival d'été de Québec and Canada Day celebrations. Historical reenactments, public yoga sessions, and food festivals are common.

In winter, the landscape turns into a snowy playground, with cross-country skiing and snowshoeing trails offering a dynamic way to explore the terrain. Seasonal installations light up parts of the park, and the occasional snowfall adds a silent reverence to the battle memorials.

The **Museum of the Plains of Abraham** provides much-needed context for the park's historical depth. Through multimedia displays and tactile exhibits, visitors learn about colonial warfare, 18th-century military life, and the socio-political consequences of the 1759 conflict. Families will appreciate the interactive components and scavenger hunts designed for children.

Rising above the plains is **The Citadel**, Québec City's proud military fortress. Its star-shaped design is modeled after European citadel plans, adapted for North American topography. The thick stone walls, guard towers, and barracks remain in use, as the site is an active military base. Yet, much of it is open to the public through guided tours.

One of the Citadel's highlights is the **Changing of the Guard** ceremony. It begins with a military band and unfolds with meticulous drills, featuring soldiers in bearskin hats and red tunics. A unique twist is the inclusion of **Batisse**, the regiment's goat mascot, a tradition borrowed from the French military and maintained with solemnity and charm.

Inside the Citadel's **Military Museum**, visitors encounter exhibits that range from Napoleonic artifacts to peacekeeping missions. Stories of bravery, sacrifice, and Canadian military evolution are told through medals, uniforms, and immersive installations.

Walking the ramparts, visitors enjoy unmatched views of the St. Lawrence River and Old Québec. The high vantage point once offered strategic defense; today it offers serene contemplation.

As a whole, the Plains of Abraham and The Citadel offer a rare convergence of landscape, legacy, and living tradition. They remind visitors that history is not confined to books or museums—it lives in the spaces we share and the stories we tell. From a decisive colonial battleground to a gathering place for modern Québec, this historic plateau continues to shape the narrative of the city, province, and nation.

3.5 Quartier Petit Champlain

A Brief Story

Tucked into the lower reaches of Old Québec, beneath the towering cliffs of Cap Diamant, **Quartier Petit Champlain** is often described as the most enchanting neighborhood in Canada. With its cobblestone streets, 17th-century stone buildings, and charming artisan boutiques, this district offers a glimpse into the earliest days of European settlement in North America. Named after Samuel de Champlain, the founder of Québec City, this neighborhood is believed to be one of the oldest commercial streets on the continent.

Historically, it served as the bustling heart of New France's port activities. Merchants, tradespeople, and craftsmen once lined the narrow streets, conducting business just steps from the St. Lawrence River. Though the district fell into decline during the industrial age, a major restoration effort in the 1970s, spearheaded by local artists and the cooperative Coopérative du Quartier Petit Champlain, revived its historic character and artisanal roots. Today, it thrives as a cultural and commercial hub that celebrates Québec's French heritage and community spirit.

Location

- **Address**: Rue du Petit-Champlain, Québec City, QC G1K 4H5, Canada
- **Proximity**: Situated in Lower Town (Basse-Ville), below the cliffs of Upper Town and near Place Royale
- **Access Points**: Via the Breakneck Stairs (Escalier Casse-Cou), the Funicular from Dufferin Terrace, or by walking from the Old Port area

Admission Price

- **Public Access**: Free to enter and explore the neighborhood
- **Individual attractions, shops, and performances**: Prices vary
- **Seasonal activities and guided walking tours**: From CAD 15 to CAD 25

Website & Contact Information

- **Website**: https://www.quartierpetitchamplain.com/en/
- **Phone**: +1 418-692-2613

Opening Hours

- **Shops and Boutiques**: Typically 10:00 AM to 6:00 PM (later during holidays and festivals)
- **Restaurants and Cafés**: 11:00 AM to 9:00 PM (varies by venue)
- **Public Spaces**: Accessible year-round, 24 hours a day
- **Seasonal Events**: Christmas Market, summer street performances, and fall art walks

Key Features

1. Rue du Petit-Champlain

The main artery of the district is lined with historic buildings housing over 45 independent shops, artist studios, and restaurants. Window boxes, stone facades, and hand-painted signs evoke the feel of a bygone European village.

2. Fresque du Petit-Champlain
A large trompe-l'œil mural depicts significant events from the neighborhood's history, showcasing fires, landslides, and historical figures that shaped the area.

3. Breakneck Stairs (Escalier Casse-Cou)
These steep stairs, among the oldest in Québec, connect Upper and Lower Town and offer excellent views of the district below.

4. Funicular Railway
Running since 1879, this glass-sided elevator offers a scenic (and accessible) alternative to the stairs, connecting Dufferin Terrace with Rue du Petit-Champlain.

5. Boutique Artisanal Scene
Shops sell handmade goods, from wool sweaters and leather bags to jewelry and blown glass—many made by local craftspeople.

6. Seasonal Decorations
The district transforms with each season: flowers in spring, street music in summer, brilliant foliage in fall, and twinkling lights and pine garlands in winter. The Christmas decor is particularly magical.

7. Le Théâtre Petit Champlain
A cozy venue for live music, theater, and comedy performances, it adds a cultural depth to the district.

8. Place Royale
Located at the northern end of the district, this historic plaza is home to Notre-Dame-des-Victoires Church and is often considered the cradle of French America.

Visitor Services

- **Tourist Information**: Available at kiosks during summer and holidays
- **Public Restrooms**: Near the funicular and in select public buildings
- **Seating & Rest Areas**: Benches along Rue du Petit-Champlain
- **Guided Tours**: History, ghost, and food tours available with bilingual guides
- **Accessibility**: While the district has cobbled paths and narrow lanes, it is largely navigable with the help of the funicular
- **Dining**: Cafés, bistros, crêperies, and regional cuisine spots
- **Artisan Demonstrations**: Some workshops offer live demonstrations
- **ATM & Currency Exchange**: Available within walking distance

Description

Quartier Petit Champlain is where Québec City's soul resides—a place where past and present merge on stone-paved streets that feel as though they were lifted from a fairy tale. Each step through this district reveals another layer of history and local life. Here, no two buildings are quite alike, and every window tells a story. French is the language of the street, but smiles speak universally.

On a summer morning, the neighborhood hums with the gentle clatter of shop shutters, the smell of croissants wafting from open doors, and the echoes of a street musician strumming a chanson. Tourists amble slowly, peering into windows of artisanal boutiques or enjoying espresso on a café patio. Artists set up easels on corners, capturing the district's timelessness in watercolor.

In the golden months of autumn, the district is draped in warm hues, and the rustic charm of its storefronts is accentuated by pumpkins, harvest wreaths, and maple-themed treats. Local merchants often decorate their storefronts in elaborate detail, offering visitors a visual feast alongside their wares.

Winter brings perhaps the most celebrated transformation. As the snow falls, Petit Champlain becomes a winter village worthy of a storybook. Icicle lights drape the eaves, and pine garlands wrap around lamp posts. The Christmas Market, set against the snow-dusted stone facades, offers mulled wine, handmade ornaments, and warm woolens. Carolers and performers bring cheer to the frosty air.

Dining here is both a pleasure and a journey. Whether it's a quiet crepe breakfast, a fondue dinner, or a Quebecois tasting menu paired with regional wine, each venue prides itself on local flavor and ambiance. Cafés often feature exposed stone interiors, wood-burning fireplaces, and intimate settings ideal for conversation.

Beyond shopping and dining, the spirit of Petit Champlain is rooted in its community of creators. Many of the artisans and business owners have lived in the area for generations. They know its stories and are happy to share them. The district's cooperative model ensures that commercialization does not overpower authenticity.

Evenings bring a different rhythm. The district slows as twilight descends. Lights twinkle in windows, the chatter of day gives way to quiet reflection, and theatergoers filter toward the Théâtre Petit Champlain for live performances. It is in these moments that the district feels suspended in time—timeless and present all at once.

Visiting Quartier Petit Champlain is not merely a shopping trip or sightseeing excursion; it is an immersion into Québec's living heritage. It rewards those who linger, who chat with a shopkeeper, who taste the jam before buying it, or who pause in a quiet courtyard to hear the bells echo from the Upper Town.

Whether under a summer sun or snowfall, it charms without trying. It is a place that touches all the senses—a touchstone for what makes Québec City not just historic, but truly magical.

3.6 Musée de la Civilisation

A Brief Story

Inaugurated in 1988 and located at the confluence of Québec's past and present in the historic Old Port district, the **Musée de la Civilisation** (Museum of Civilization) stands as one of Canada's most important and engaging cultural institutions. Designed by renowned architect Moshe Safdie, the museum seamlessly integrates contemporary architectural lines with preserved historical buildings, symbolizing its mission: to explore the intersection of human identity, societal development, and cultural expression.

Rather than functioning as a traditional history museum locked in the past, the Musée de la Civilisation has always embraced a dynamic, multidisciplinary approach to storytelling. It dives into local Québécois heritage while placing it in conversation with global cultures, modern science, anthropology, and contemporary issues. Its thoughtful curation, interactive exhibits, and immersive environments have made it a favorite among locals, families, scholars, and international travelers alike.

Location

- **Address**: 85 Rue Dalhousie, Québec City, QC G1K 8R2, Canada
- **Proximity**: Located in Lower Town (Basse-Ville), a short walk from Quartier Petit Champlain and Place Royale
- **Situated along**: The St. Lawrence River, near the Old Port and marina

Admission Price

- **Adults**: CAD 22
- **Seniors (65+)**: CAD 20
- **Students**: CAD 14
- **Children (11 and under)**: Free
- **Family Package**: CAD 44 (2 adults + 3 children)
- **Annual Membership**: Available with additional perks

Website & Contact Information

- **Website**: https://www.mcq.org
- **Phone**: +1 418-643-2158

Opening Hours

- **Tuesday to Sunday**: 10:00 AM to 5:00 PM
- **Monday**: Closed (except holidays and summer months)
- **Special evening events**: Occasionally open late for lectures, performances, and exhibits

Key Features

1. Temporary & Rotating Exhibits

A hallmark of the museum is its constantly evolving program of temporary exhibitions. Topics range from global civilizations, ancient rituals, and Indigenous storytelling to modern design, digital futures, and pop culture.

2. Permanent Exhibit: "People of Québec... Then and Now"

This flagship gallery presents the complex, layered history of Québec through personal narratives, multimedia storytelling, and historical artifacts. It celebrates both the triumphs and challenges of the province's evolution.

3. Indigenous Voices and Perspectives

A strong commitment to First Nations and Inuit heritage is evident in exhibits co-created with Indigenous communities. These spaces focus on traditions, worldviews, resilience, and modern-day realities.

4. Interactive Learning Zones

Especially popular among families, these zones allow visitors to engage with science, nature, and history through hands-on activities and experiments.

5. Architecture & Design

The building itself is a marvel: exposed stone walls from original structures meet expansive glass walls and fluid interior spaces. Safdie's vision offers beautiful natural light and symbolic transparency.

6. Themed Programming

Includes film screenings, expert talks, workshops, and guided tours that align with current exhibits.

7. Multilingual Accessibility

All exhibits feature signage in French and English, with some audio guides and video content available in additional languages.

8. On-site Auditorium

Used for live performances, lectures, symposiums, and cultural events.

9. Boutique and Gift Shop

Offers a curated selection of books, artisan crafts, Indigenous art, educational toys, and exhibit-themed souvenirs.

10. Café 47

A scenic cafeteria with locally sourced meals, coffees, and river views, ideal for a relaxing interlude during your visit.

Visitor Services

- **Accessibility**: Fully wheelchair accessible, with ramps, elevators, and adapted restrooms

- **Guided Tours**: Available in French and English, including private group tours by reservation
- **Audio Guides**: Offered in multiple languages for select exhibits
- **Free Wi-Fi**: Available throughout the building
- **Restrooms**: Clean and available on every level
- **Lockers & Coat Check**: Secure storage for bags and personal items
- **Educational Materials**: Curriculum-aligned content for school visits and families
- **Event Rentals**: Select halls and rooms available for cultural events, weddings, and conferences

Description

The Musée de la Civilisation invites visitors into a thoughtfully curated world where the stories of humankind are explored in surprising and emotionally resonant ways. Rather than focusing solely on static displays, the museum excels at engaging the mind and heart alike, using design, technology, and narrative to breathe life into the objects and ideas on display.

Upon entering, guests are greeted by a spacious atrium bathed in natural light. The layout of the museum promotes intuitive exploration—each wing beckons with unique lighting, sounds, and visuals, setting the stage for immersive discovery. Throughout the galleries, curated soundscapes, motion-activated displays, and tactile installations encourage active participation.

A walk through the permanent "People of Québec... Then and Now" exhibit is a highlight. It charts the region's story from the time of the Indigenous peoples, through colonization and industrialization, into modern-day Québec. Visitors encounter letters from early settlers, maps etched by explorers, protest banners from social movements, and interviews with modern citizens. It's a living timeline, grounded in personal voices and real struggles.

Equally compelling are the Indigenous-led exhibits. These are not mere displays of artifacts, but platforms for dialogue. Co-curated with Indigenous communities, they often include contemporary artwork, video testimonials, and spiritual symbolism. These sections respectfully challenge conventional museum narratives, giving First Nations and Inuit peoples agency over their representation.

The museum's temporary exhibitions range widely in topic and tone. Past highlights include in-depth explorations of Ancient Egypt, futuristic robotics, fashion history, and the social dynamics of food. Each exhibit offers hands-on components, making them ideal for all ages.

For families, the interactive zones are a major draw. Young visitors can roleplay historical scenes, solve science puzzles, or build their own digital civilizations. Special family programs during school holidays and summer ensure a full day of engaging activities.

The museum also plays a central role in Québec City's intellectual and artistic scene. Regular lectures from anthropologists, historians, artists, and thought leaders make it a hub for lifelong learning. During Nuit des Musées and other cultural festivals, the Musée stays open late and offers exclusive programming.

A stroll through the museum reveals not just the diversity of human experience but also the interconnectedness of culture, environment, and identity. Exhibits are not only educational but empathetic—often prompting visitors to reflect on their own lives and communities.

Whether you spend two hours or an entire day, the Musée de la Civilisation ensures that you leave enriched, informed, and inspired. It is a must-visit for travelers seeking meaningful cultural engagement and a deeper understanding of the vibrant world around them. The museum reflects Québec's commitment to preserving history while embracing the future, making it not just a top attraction but a cornerstone of the city's intellectual and emotional life.

3.7 Basilica of Sainte-Anne-de-Beaupré

A Brief Story

The **Basilica of Sainte-Anne-de-Beaupré**, located just 30 kilometers northeast of Québec City, is more than a place of worship—it is a revered spiritual destination with deep roots in North American Catholicism. Dedicated to **Saint Anne**, the grandmother of Jesus Christ, the basilica has drawn **pilgrims and visitors for over 350 years**, making it one of the oldest and most visited pilgrimage sites in North America.

The story begins in 1658, when a humble chapel was constructed by early French settlers along the banks of the St. Lawrence River. Legend has it that during construction, a crippled worker was miraculously healed, marking the beginning of countless reported miracles attributed to the intercession of Saint Anne. As word spread, more pilgrims came seeking hope and healing.

Over the centuries, several chapels and churches were built on the site, each larger and more elaborate than the last. The current basilica, completed in **1923**, is the fifth church to occupy the site and stands as a **masterpiece of Romanesque Revival architecture**, offering visitors a blend of sacred tradition, artistic grandeur, and peaceful reflection.

Location

- **Address**: 10018 Avenue Royale, Sainte-Anne-de-Beaupré, QC G0A 3C0, Canada
- **Distance from Québec City**: Approximately 30 km (30–35 minutes by car or bus)
- **Situated along**: Route de la Nouvelle-France (Avenue Royale), a scenic heritage route

Admission Price

- **General Admission**: Free
- **Suggested Donation**: Voluntary contributions are welcome to support upkeep and operations
- **Museum Entry (optional)**: CAD 5
- **Group Tours**: Fees may apply depending on guide and duration

Website & Contact Information

- **Website**: https://sanctuairesainteanne.org
- **Phone**: +1 418-827-3781
- **Email**: info@sanctuairesainteanne.org

Opening Hours

- **Basilica**: Open daily, typically from 8:30 AM to 5:00 PM
- **Gift Shop and Museum**: 9:00 AM to 5:00 PM (seasonal variations apply)
- **Mass and Confession**: Multiple services held daily; special schedules during feast days

Key Features

1. Interior Frescoes and Mosaics
The basilica's interior is richly adorned with vibrant frescoes, gold-leaf mosaics, and

intricate stained glass. These artworks depict scenes from the life of Saint Anne, the Virgin Mary, and Christ, offering visual narratives steeped in faith and devotion.

2. The Pillars of Crutches

At the entrance, two towering columns are lined with crutches, canes, and orthopedic braces left behind by pilgrims reportedly healed after praying to Saint Anne. This deeply moving visual testifies to the site's enduring spiritual significance.

3. The Great Organ and Sacred Music

A magnificent Casavant organ fills the basilica with sacred music during liturgies and concerts. The basilica's acoustics make it a favorite for both religious and classical performances.

4. The Crypt Church

Beneath the main basilica lies the Crypt Church, a quieter, more intimate space used for weekday Masses and personal prayer. Its stone walls and candle-lit chapels create a solemn, contemplative ambiance.

5. Scala Sancta (Holy Stairs)

Modeled after the staircase in Rome believed to have been climbed by Christ during his Passion, the Scala Sancta here is climbed by pilgrims on their knees in acts of penance and devotion.

6. The Way of the Cross

An outdoor path with 14 life-sized bronze Stations of the Cross winds up the hillside behind the basilica. The scenic and spiritual walk culminates in sweeping views of the St. Lawrence River.

7. Saint Anne's Fountain

A decorative fountain believed by some pilgrims to have healing properties is located near the basilica's entrance. Pilgrims often collect water here or use it in acts of prayer and reflection.

8. Annual Pilgrimage and Feast Day

Held on **July 26**, the Feast of Saint Anne draws thousands of visitors each year for special Masses, processions, and blessings.

9. Basilica Museum

Exhibits here include liturgical vestments, devotional items, historical documents, and artifacts related to Saint Anne and the site's history.

10. Stained Glass Windows

Dozens of ornate windows flood the basilica with colored light, portraying Biblical stories, saints, and scenes from Québec's Catholic heritage.

Visitor Services

- **Free Parking**: Ample space for cars and buses
- **Gift Shop**: Offers religious items, medals, rosaries, books, and local artisanal crafts
- **Pilgrimage Services**: Assistance with organizing group visits, including spiritual guidance and accommodation nearby
- **Café and Snack Bar**: Seasonal refreshments available onsite
- **Restrooms**: Located near the basilica and museum
- **Wheelchair Access**: Most of the basilica and paths are accessible
- **Interpretive Panels**: Multilingual signage throughout the grounds

Description

The Basilica of Sainte-Anne-de-Beaupré is not only a spiritual sanctuary but a living museum of faith, culture, and community. Every stone and sculpture tells a story of devotion that spans continents and centuries. For believers, it is a place of pilgrimage and prayer; for others, it is a cultural and architectural treasure.

Walking into the basilica, visitors are enveloped in serenity. The soaring arches and vaulted ceilings lead the eye heavenward, while gentle music or quiet chanting often fills the space. The scent of incense lingers in the air, mingling with the soft rustle of candle flames. It is a place designed not only to impress but to invite reflection and inner peace.

The **pillars of crutches** are particularly impactful—an unspoken archive of healing and gratitude that strikes visitors with its authenticity. Each crutch or cane represents someone who arrived with pain and left with hope. Nearby, quiet chapels allow visitors to light candles, say prayers, or sit in contemplative silence.

As you explore further, the **Crypt Church** offers a quieter, more personal setting. Its cool stone interiors and subdued lighting make it ideal for personal devotions. Visitors often leave handwritten intentions at the small side altars, adding to the sense of communal hope and support.

Outside, the **Way of the Cross** trail leads uphill through forested grounds, passing stations that depict Christ's journey to Calvary. The natural setting adds to the spiritual atmosphere, and the view at the summit is both a physical and symbolic reward.

The **Scala Sancta**, while less well known, is powerful in its simplicity. Watching pilgrims climb its steps on their knees is a testament to enduring faith and human humility. It offers a rare glimpse into living spiritual practice in a modern world.

Even for non-religious visitors, the basilica offers rich rewards. Architecturally, the building is a masterwork of stone, glass, and wood. The stained-glass windows alone merit a slow, thoughtful walk. Lit by the afternoon sun, they dazzle with colors that shift and dance across the floor.

The **museum**, though modest in size, offers insights into both the ecclesiastical and local heritage. It places the basilica in the wider context of Québec's colonial and religious history, highlighting its enduring importance in the lives of believers from all walks of life.

Throughout the year, special services, concerts, and public events breathe life into the space. From organ recitals and visiting choirs to major religious festivals, the basilica serves as both a house of God and a community gathering place.

In every season, Sainte-Anne-de-Beaupré offers something new. In winter, the snow lends a quiet solemnity. In spring, flowers bloom around the base of the shrine. Summer brings vibrant processions, and fall wraps the grounds in golden foliage.

Whether you're seeking spiritual renewal, historical insight, or architectural beauty, the Basilica of Sainte-Anne-de-Beaupré is a journey well worth taking. It is a sanctuary not just of faith, but of human dignity, hope, and the power of tradition that continues to inspire across generations.

Chapter 4. Best Accommodation Options

4.1 Luxury Hotels & Historic Inns

Québec City's most distinguished hotels not only offer top-tier amenities and service, but also immerse guests in the city's storied past and elegant charm. From grand châteaus perched over the St. Lawrence River to immaculately restored inns nestled in cobblestone lanes, these accommodations exemplify heritage, comfort, and sophistication.

1. Fairmont Le Château Frontenac

- **Price Range**: From CAD 450 to CAD 900+ per night (varies by room and season)
- **Address**: 1 Rue des Carrières, Québec City, QC G1R 4P5, Canada
- **Contact**: +1 418-692-3861 | chateaufrontenac@fairmont.com

- **Website**: https://www.fairmont.com/frontenac-quebec/
- **Location**: Old Québec (Upper Town), overlooking Dufferin Terrace and the St. Lawrence River

Key Features:

- Iconic castle-style architecture and a UNESCO-adjacent location
- Over 600 rooms and suites with historic charm and modern amenities
- Award-winning spa (Moment Spa), indoor pool, and fitness center
- Fine dining at Champlain Restaurant, Bistro Le Sam, and 1608 Wine & Cheese Bar

Visitor Services:

- Valet parking, concierge, room service
- Multilingual staff, business center, babysitting services
- Pet-friendly rooms available
- Guided historical tours of the hotel available to guests

2. Auberge Saint-Antoine

- **Price Range**: CAD 375 to CAD 800 per night
- **Address**: 8 Rue Saint-Antoine, Québec City, QC G1K 4C9, Canada
- **Contact**: +1 418-692-2211 | info@saint-antoine.com
- **Website**: https://www.saint-antoine.com
- **Location**: Old Port (Vieux-Port), near the Museum of Civilization and Quartier Petit Champlain

Key Features:

- Boutique Relais & Châteaux hotel integrating historical artifacts in its décor
- Stylish rooms and suites with luxury linens, heated bathroom floors, and river or courtyard views
- In-house restaurant Chez Muffy, located in an 1822 maritime warehouse
- On-site cinema room and state-of-the-art gym

Visitor Services:

- Complimentary valet and concierge services
- Full-service spa and massage therapy
- Daily housekeeping and turn-down service
- Business facilities and event hosting available

3. Hotel Manoir Victoria

- **Price Range**: CAD 275 to CAD 600 per night
- **Address**: 44 Côte du Palais, Québec City, QC G1R 4H8, Canada
- **Contact**: +1 418-692-1030 | info@manoir-victoria.com
- **Website**: https://www.manoir-victoria.com
- **Location**: Inside Old Québec's fortified walls, near Rue Saint-Jean and Place d'Armes

Key Features:

- Contemporary design within a heritage façade
- 156 rooms including deluxe and executive suites
- Gourmet Nordic cuisine at Chez Boulay – Bistro Boréal
- Heated indoor pool and Scandinavian-style sauna

Visitor Services:

- Valet parking and full-service front desk
- Dry cleaning and luggage storage
- Accessibility features for guests with reduced mobility
- Meeting rooms and business center on-site

4. Le Germain Hotel Québec

- **Price Range**: CAD 320 to CAD 650 per night
- **Address**: 126 Rue Saint-Pierre, Québec City, QC G1K 4A8, Canada
- **Contact**: +1 418-692-2224 | quebec@germainhotels.com
- **Website**: https://www.germainhotels.com
- **Location**: Lower Town (Basse-Ville), a short walk from the Old Port and Quartier Petit Champlain

Key Features:

- Elegant boutique atmosphere with exposed stone walls and modern comforts
- 60 luxurious rooms featuring Egyptian cotton bedding and Nespresso machines
- Eco-friendly operations and locally sourced breakfast
- Cozy lounge and small library for guests

Visitor Services:

- Personalized concierge and valet service
- Fitness room and conference facilities

- Free Wi-Fi and complimentary breakfast included
- Dog-friendly with prior arrangement

5. Monastère des Augustines

- **Price Range**: CAD 200 to CAD 450 per night (health-conscious, minimalist stays)
- **Address**: 77 Rue des Remparts, Québec City, QC G1R 0C3, Canada
- **Contact**: +1 418-694-1639 | info@monastere.ca
- **Website**: https://www.monastere.ca
- **Location**: Inside a 17th-century monastery in Old Québec

Key Features:

- Wellness-focused heritage hotel offering restful stays in a historic convent
- Rooms with monastic simplicity or contemporary amenities
- Wellness center with yoga, meditation, and holistic health services
- Organic cuisine and silent breakfast options

Visitor Services:

- Cultural programming and access to museum exhibits on site
- Library and reading rooms
- Multilingual staff and guided meditative walks
- Ideal for solo travelers, wellness retreats, and quiet stays

Each of these luxurious accommodations brings a distinct flavor to the Québec City experience. Whether you prefer regal grandeur, understated elegance, or peaceful wellness, these top-tier options provide not only a place to stay but a meaningful extension of the city's rich cultural and historical narrative.

4.2 Mid-Range Hotels & Boutique Stays

For travelers seeking a balance between comfort, location, and value, Quebec City offers an excellent selection of mid-range hotels and boutique accommodations. These properties often combine historic charm with modern conveniences, making them ideal for couples, solo explorers, and families alike. Below are some of the most prominent mid-range and boutique stays in Quebec City:

Hotel Manoir Victoria

- **Price Range:** $180–$260 CAD per night (varies by season and room type)
- **Address:** 44 Côte du Palais, Quebec City, QC G1R 4H8

- **Contact:** +1 418-692-1030 | info@manoirvictoria.com
- **Location:** Old Quebec (Upper Town), within walking distance of historic landmarks
- **Website:** www.manoirvictoria.com

Key Features:

- Indoor heated pool and sauna
- Fitness centre
- On-site fine-dining restaurant (Chez Boulay – Bistro Boréal)
- Free Wi-Fi and business center
- Elegant decor blending heritage and modern style

Visitor Services:

- Multilingual concierge service
- Valet parking (fee applies)
- Pet-friendly options available
- Laundry and dry-cleaning services

Overview:

Set in the heart of Old Quebec, Hotel Manoir Victoria is a classic 4-star boutique property with a warm, contemporary atmosphere. Ideal for both leisure and business travelers, it offers easy access to the Old City's cobbled streets, shops, and historic sites. The charming interior design is a nod to Quebec's European influences, while the staff is known for their attention to detail and helpful local recommendations.

Auberge Place d'Armes

- **Price Range:** $190–$240 CAD per night
- **Address:** 24 Rue Sainte-Anne, Quebec City, QC G1R 3X3
- **Contact:** +1 418-694-9485 | info@aubergeplacedarmes.com
- **Location:** Directly across from Château Frontenac in Old Quebec
- **Website:** www.aubergeplacedarmes.com

Key Features:

- Historic 17th-century architecture
- Individually styled rooms with exposed brick walls
- In-room Nespresso machines and rain showers
- On-site French bistro

Visitor Services:

- Personalized concierge service
- Airport transfer (additional cost)
- Room service available during bistro hours
- Bilingual staff

Overview:
Auberge Place d'Armes blends history with charm in one of the most coveted locations in Quebec City. With only a handful of rooms, it provides an intimate experience with stylish furnishings and thoughtful touches. The inn's boutique nature ensures personalized service and an immersive stay steps away from the city's most famous attractions.

Hotel le Priori

- **Price Range:** $170–$230 CAD per night
- **Address:** 15 Rue du Sault-au-Matelot, Quebec City, QC G1K 3Y7
- **Contact:** +1 418-692-3992 | info@hotellepriori.com
- **Location:** Lower Town (Petit-Champlain district), near the Old Port
- **Website:** www.hotellepriori.com

Key Features:

- Former residence of architect Jean Baillairgé
- Art-deco design and loft-style suites
- Some rooms with private terraces or fireplaces
- Complimentary continental breakfast

Visitor Services:

- Concierge and tour booking assistance
- Elevator access to all floors
- Business facilities and high-speed internet
- Multilingual front desk

Overview:

Hotel le Priori offers a creative, art-focused lodging experience in the heart of Quebec's Lower Town. It's popular among design lovers and couples seeking a romantic escape. With spacious rooms and stylish interiors, this boutique hotel is tucked into a quiet lane near excellent dining and the charming Quartier Petit Champlain.

Hotel du Vieux-Québec

- **Price Range:** $160–$210 CAD per night
- **Address:** 1190 Rue Saint-Jean, Quebec City, QC G1R 1S6
- **Contact:** +1 418-692-1850 | info@hvq.com
- **Location:** Old Quebec, on Rue Saint-Jean
- **Website:** www.hvq.com

Key Features:

- Eco-friendly operations and rooftop garden
- Rustic-chic design with hardwood floors and stone walls
- On-site farm-to-table restaurant (Tournebroche)
- Netflix-enabled smart TVs

Visitor Services:

- Free bicycle rentals in warmer months
- Picnic baskets delivered to your room
- Free Wi-Fi and public computers in lobby
- Library and common lounge

Overview:

A beloved mid-range option that's big on sustainability and charm, Hotel du Vieux-Québec delivers a unique blend of comfort and conscience. From organic toiletries to curated art and local produce, every detail is thoughtfully selected. It's a popular base for travelers who want a feel-good stay in the heart of the Old City.

4.3 Budget-Friendly Lodgings

Travelers exploring Quebec City on a modest budget need not sacrifice comfort or convenience. The city offers several budget-friendly accommodations that provide excellent service, prime locations, and charming atmospheres. Whether you're a backpacker, student, or simply looking to stretch your travel funds, these prominent budget options combine affordability with character.

Auberge Internationale de Québec

- **Price Range:** $40–$130 CAD per night (dorms and private rooms available)
- **Address:** 19 Rue Sainte-Ursule, Quebec City, QC G1R 4E1
- **Contact:** +1 418-694-0755 | info@hostellingquebec.com
- **Location:** Old Quebec (Upper Town), just steps from Château Frontenac

- **Website:** www.hostellingquebec.com

Key Features:

- Largest hostel in North America
- Shared dormitories and private rooms
- Historic building with modern upgrades
- Communal kitchen and dining area

Visitor Services:

- Free Wi-Fi
- On-site bar and café
- Laundry facilities and bike storage
- Social activities and walking tours

Overview:

A favorite among international backpackers, Auberge Internationale de Québec offers a vibrant, youthful atmosphere in a prime location. Housed in a charming heritage building, the hostel attracts solo travelers, students, and groups. The shared kitchen and lively common areas make it easy to meet fellow adventurers, and the proximity to major attractions makes it an unbeatable value.

Hotel Terrasse Dufferin

- **Price Range:** $85–$150 CAD per night
- **Address:** 6 Rue de la Terrasse-Dufferin, Quebec City, QC G1R 4N5
- **Contact:** +1 418-694-9471 | info@terrasse-dufferin.com
- **Location:** Just beside Dufferin Terrace, overlooking the St. Lawrence River
- **Website:** www.terrasse-dufferin.com

Key Features:

- Victorian-style heritage home
- Many rooms with river views
- Quaint décor with antique furnishings
- Family-owned and operated

Visitor Services:

- Free continental breakfast
- Limited parking (additional cost)
- Multilingual staff

- Luggage storage available

Overview:

Hotel Terrasse Dufferin offers a cozy, old-world ambiance that suits budget-conscious travelers seeking an authentic Quebec experience. Located near one of the city's most iconic boardwalks, it boasts exceptional views and walkable access to museums, cafés, and the Château Frontenac. The personal attention from the family-run staff is a highlight for many return guests.

Hôtel Cap Diamant

- **Price Range:** $120–$160 CAD per night
- **Address:** 39 Avenue Sainte-Geneviève, Quebec City, QC G1R 4B3
- **Contact:** +1 418-694-0313 | info@capdiamant.com
- **Location:** On a quiet residential street in Old Quebec, near the Citadelle
- **Website:** www.capdiamant.com

Key Features:

- Quaint 19th-century townhouse
- Personalized rooms with antique décor
- Complimentary breakfast included
- Peaceful garden terrace

Visitor Services:

- Concierge recommendations for local dining
- In-room coffee makers and mini-fridges
- Daily housekeeping
- Free Wi-Fi

Overview:

This quiet and affordable boutique inn is a hidden gem for travelers who appreciate charm and tranquility. Hôtel Cap Diamant's central location allows you to walk to most major attractions, yet its peaceful ambiance makes it perfect for a restful stay. The property's classic interior, high ceilings, and friendly service make it stand out among budget choices.

Hotel du Nord

- **Price Range:** $100–$140 CAD per night
- **Address:** 640 Rue Saint-Vallier Ouest, Quebec City, QC G1N 1C5
- **Contact:** +1 418-522-1375 | info@hotelquebecnord.com

- **Location:** Saint-Sauveur district, about 10 minutes from Old Quebec by car or bus
- **Website:** www.hotelquebecnord.com

Key Features:

- Indoor pool and fitness room
- Modern rooms with kitchenette options
- Breakfast available on-site
- Free parking

Visitor Services:

- 24-hour front desk
- Tour and ticket assistance
- Business centre and computer access
- Laundry service

Overview:

Ideal for travelers who don't mind staying slightly outside the historic center, Hotel du Nord offers clean, spacious rooms with practical amenities at an attractive price. The location provides easy access to public transport, making it a great option for families or budget travelers with their own vehicle.

4.4 Unique Stays: B&Bs, Cabins & Apartment Rentals

For travelers looking to immerse themselves more personally in Quebec City's historic charm, culture, and hospitality, unique stays such as cozy bed-and-breakfasts, rustic cabins, and thoughtfully curated apartment rentals provide an unforgettable alternative to traditional hotels. These lodgings offer a deeper connection to the city's neighborhoods, often blending historic architecture with intimate service and homely comforts. Below are some of the most prominent and highly regarded options in this category.

Maison Historique James Thompson (B&B)

- **Price Range:** $140–$180 CAD per night (includes breakfast)
- **Address:** 47 Rue Sainte-Ursule, Quebec City, QC G1R 4E4
- **Contact:** +1 418-694-1884 | info@james-thompson.com
- **Location:** Upper Old Quebec, steps from historic landmarks
- **Website:** www.james-thompson.com

Key Features:

- Historic 200-year-old home with original stonework
- Antique furnishings and cozy, personalized decor
- Award-winning homemade breakfasts served daily
- Small garden patio

Visitor Services:

- Warm, personalized service from on-site hosts
- Free Wi-Fi
- Private ensuite bathrooms
- Secure luggage storage

Overview:

This charming bed-and-breakfast offers a slice of 19th-century Quebec with a warm, familial touch. Located within walking distance of Château Frontenac and the Citadelle, the James Thompson House is known for its attention to detail, friendly hospitality, and delectable homemade morning fare. It's ideal for couples and history enthusiasts who appreciate quiet, character-filled lodgings.

Le Gîte du Quartier des Arts (B&B)

- **Price Range:** $130–$165 CAD per night
- **Address:** 51 Rue Crémazie, Quebec City, QC G1R 1X4
- **Contact:** +1 418-523-1555 | info@gitedesarts.com
- **Location:** Montcalm District, near the Musée national des beaux-arts
- **Website:** www.gitedesarts.com

Key Features:

- Eclectic, art-inspired interiors
- Home-cooked breakfasts featuring local products
- Walking distance to shops, galleries, and restaurants
- Intimate, quiet environment

Visitor Services:

- Bilingual hosts
- Shared common areas and reading room
- Tourist guidance and recommendations
- Free Wi-Fi

Overview:

Nestled in the city's arts district, this creative B&B offers a unique and relaxed alternative to central hotels. Guests will appreciate the personal touches, colorful decor, and the cultural flair of the surrounding Montcalm neighborhood. It's perfect for travelers looking to enjoy the city's quieter, more local side while remaining close to major attractions.

Les Lofts 1048 (Apartment Rentals)

- **Price Range:** $180–$260 CAD per night (based on size and season)
- **Address:** 1048 Rue Saint-Jean, Quebec City, QC G1R 1R6
- **Contact:** +1 418-431-9905 | info@leslofts1048.com
- **Location:** In the heart of Old Quebec, along Rue Saint-Jean
- **Website:** www.leslofts1048.com

Key Features:

- Modern, fully-equipped apartments in a restored heritage building
- Kitchens, laundry, and living spaces in every unit
- Stylish interiors with large windows and high ceilings
- Elevator access and self-check-in

Visitor Services:

- Contactless entry
- Concierge assistance by phone
- Secure access and 24/7 guest support
- Ideal for long stays or families

Overview:

Perfect for travelers who prefer independence and space, Les Lofts 1048 offers all the comforts of home with a front-row seat to Quebec City's most vibrant pedestrian street. The lofts are a popular choice for families, digital nomads, or small groups who appreciate cooking their own meals, having laundry on hand, and exploring the city like a local.

Le Chalet du Faubourg (Cabin Rental)

- **Price Range:** $150–$190 CAD per night
- **Address:** 225 Rue Saint-Paul, Quebec City, QC G1K 3W2
- **Contact:** +1 418-694-9907 | chalet@faubourg.com
- **Location:** Old Port district, just outside Old Quebec's lower town
- **Website:** www.chaletdufaubourg.com

Key Features:

- Rustic-style cabin aesthetic in an urban setting
- Full kitchen, fireplace, and wood interiors
- Quiet residential surroundings with riverside access nearby
- Ideal for small families or couples

Visitor Services:

- Private entrance
- Free parking
- Local maps and guidebooks provided
- Self-catering facilities

Overview:

Le Chalet du Faubourg provides a serene retreat while still being within walking distance of Old Quebec's bustling shops and eateries. It delivers the ambiance of a mountain escape with the convenience of city amenities. Guests often rave about the cozy feel, privacy, and the unique experience of staying in a standalone wooden chalet within a historic urban port zone.

Monastère des Augustines (Wellness & Heritage Stay)

- **Price Range:** $160–$210 CAD per night
- **Address:** 77 Rue des Remparts, Quebec City, QC G1R 0C3
- **Contact:** +1 418-694-1639 | info@monastere.ca
- **Location:** Old Quebec, near the Fortifications
- **Website:** www.monastere.ca

Key Features:

- Converted 17th-century monastery with minimalist rooms
- Wellness-focused atmosphere (yoga, meditation, spa treatments)
- On-site museum and restaurant with health-conscious menus
- Silent corridors and historical exhibitions

Visitor Services:

- Guided tours and cultural programming
- Organic breakfast included
- Holistic wellness packages available
- Multilingual staff

Overview:
 The Monastère des Augustines is more than a place to sleep—it's an immersive spiritual and wellness retreat grounded in centuries of healing history. Guests can sleep in restored nun's quarters or contemporary rooms, participate in yoga classes, and explore a living museum dedicated to the site's religious heritage. Ideal for solo travelers, writers, or anyone craving inner peace.

Chapter 5. Food & Drink in Québec City

5.1 Traditional Québécois Cuisine

Québec City's culinary identity is deeply rooted in its French-Canadian heritage, seasonal ingredients, and rustic traditions. Traditional Québécois cuisine reflects centuries of adaptation to harsh winters, colonial influences, and a culture of comfort and celebration. Today, visitors can enjoy classic dishes passed down through generations, often reinvented with modern twists by innovative chefs who continue to honor their roots.

Below are some of the most iconic dishes, ingredients, and places where you can enjoy authentic Québécois food in Québec City.

Signature Dishes of Traditional Québécois Cuisine

Tourtière (Meat Pie)

A beloved staple, tourtière is a savory pie made from minced pork, beef, or veal (sometimes all three), seasoned with clove, cinnamon, and nutmeg. Traditionally served during the holidays, particularly Christmas and New Year's Eve, tourtière is now available in many local eateries year-round.

Where to Try It:

- *Aux Anciens Canadiens* (34 Rue Saint-Louis)
- *La Bûche* (49 Rue Saint-Louis)

Pouding Chômeur (Poor Man's Pudding)

This humble yet delicious dessert originated during the Great Depression. Made with simple ingredients like cake batter and a rich maple syrup or caramel sauce poured over it before baking, it's a warm, sweet treat often served with cream or ice cream.

Where to Try It:

- *Cochon Dingue* (46 Boulevard Champlain or other locations)
- *Chez Boulay – Bistro Boréal* (1110 Rue Saint-Jean)

Cipaille (Sea Pie)

A layered meat pie, cipaille combines various cuts of game, poultry, and pork (or beef), cooked slowly in a thick, hearty crust. Though less common on daily menus, it appears during seasonal menus and special events.

Where to Try It:

- *Aux Anciens Canadiens* often features this during holiday months
- *Seasonal pop-ups or food festivals*

Fèves au Lard (Baked Beans with Pork and Maple Syrup)

This dish combines navy beans slow-cooked with salted pork and maple syrup, resulting in a comforting, slightly sweet flavor. It's a fixture of sugar shack meals and traditional breakfasts.

Where to Try It:

- *La Bûche*

- *Buffet de l'Antiquaire* (95 Rue Saint-Paul)

Cretons

Cretons is a pork spread made with onions, spices, and breadcrumbs. Served cold on toast, it's a classic item at any authentic Québec breakfast table.

Where to Try It:

- *Le Petit Coin Latin* (69 Rue Saint-Louis)
- *Buffet de l'Antiquaire*

Key Ingredients & Cultural Influences

Traditional Québécois cuisine leans heavily on hearty ingredients, including:

- **Maple syrup** (used in both savory and sweet dishes)
- **Root vegetables** like turnips, carrots, and potatoes
- **Game meats** such as deer, rabbit, and wild fowl
- **Cured pork** and salted meats
- **Freshwater fish** like trout and walleye

Much of the cooking is slow and rustic, meant to be enjoyed communally. Recipes are often tied to religious, seasonal, or family celebrations.

Sugar Shacks (Cabanes à Sucre)

Sugar shacks are an essential part of traditional Québécois food culture, especially in spring. These rustic wooden cabins located near maple groves serve multi-course feasts featuring pea soup, baked beans, pork rinds, maple-glazed ham, and pancakes drowned in fresh maple syrup.

Nearby Sugar Shacks:

- **Erablière le Chemin du Roy** (about 30 mins from downtown Québec)
- **Cabane à Pierre** (in Frampton, slightly farther but authentic)

Many operate seasonally (March–April), but some offer year-round dining experiences or themed events.

Where to Enjoy Traditional Québécois Cuisine in Québec City

Aux Anciens Canadiens

- *Address:* 34 Rue Saint-Louis
- *Atmosphere:* Housed in one of the oldest buildings in the city
- *Specialties:* Tourtière, cipaille, maple desserts
- *Notes:* Offers fixed-price menus with generous portions

La Bûche

- *Address:* 49 Rue Saint-Louis
- *Atmosphere:* Rustic-chic and modern take on sugar shack dining
- *Specialties:* Baked beans, cretons, pouding chômeur
- *Notes:* Known for its Québec folk music and quirky interior

Buffet de l'Antiquaire

- *Address:* 95 Rue Saint-Paul
- *Atmosphere:* Casual and local-favorite diner-style eatery
- *Specialties:* Breakfasts with cretons, pea soup, meatloaf
- *Notes:* Great for early risers and hearty morning meals

Chez Boulay – Bistro Boréal

- *Address:* 1110 Rue Saint-Jean
- *Atmosphere:* Refined Nordic-inspired Québécois dining
- *Specialties:* Game meats, foraged herbs, maple-accented dishes
- *Notes:* Perfect for foodies who appreciate farm-to-table dining

Food Tours & Culinary Experiences

To dive deeper into Québec City's culinary heritage, several guided tours combine storytelling with delicious sampling.

Local Food Tours – Old Québec City Tour

- *Duration:* ~2.5 hours
- *Highlights:* Visit 5+ local restaurants and shops
- *Includes:* Tastings of local cheese, maple treats, tourtière, and cider
- *Website:* localfoodtours.com

Cicérone Tours – Flavors of Old Québec

- *Duration:* Half-day
- *Focus:* Traditional ingredients, artisanal producers, and Québécois customs
- *Includes:* Historical context and tastings
- *Website:* tourscicerone.com

5.2 Top Restaurants & Local Favorites

Québec City's vibrant culinary scene offers a rich tapestry of dining experiences, from intimate neighborhood bistros and time-honored institutions to modern fine dining and chef-driven seasonal menus. With its deep French roots and ever-evolving local food culture, the city has become one of Canada's most celebrated gastronomic destinations.

Whether you're seeking refined Quebecois cuisine, inventive farm-to-table dishes, or a cozy eatery beloved by locals, the following restaurants stand out for their quality, atmosphere, and culinary authenticity.

1. Chez Muffy

Type: Fine Dining | Farm-to-Table French-Canadian
Address: 10 Rue Saint-Antoine, Québec City, QC G1K 4C9
Contact: +1 418-692-1022 | reservations@saint-antoine.com
Website: www.saint-antoine.com/chez-muffy
Price Range: $$$

Key Features:

- Located inside Auberge Saint-Antoine, a Relais & Châteaux hotel
- 19th-century warehouse setting with wooden beams and riverside views
- Locally sourced ingredients from their own farm on Île d'Orléans

Overview:
Chez Muffy delivers a seasonal, contemporary take on traditional Quebecois cuisine in one of the city's most beautiful waterfront dining rooms. With a menu that changes regularly, dishes emphasize regional flavors, organic meats, and in-house preservation techniques.

2. Légende – Cuisine Boréale

Type: Modern Quebecois | Boreal Cuisine
Address: 255 Rue Saint-Paul, Québec City, QC G1K 3W5
Contact: +1 418-614-2555
Website: www.restoboreale.com
Price Range: $$$

Key Features:

- Focus on Nordic-inspired cuisine with boreal forest ingredients
- Sleek minimalist design with an open kitchen
- Tasting menu and à la carte options available

Overview:
Légende is a culinary love letter to the land and forest of Quebec. Expect wild herbs, roots, game meats, and seafood prepared with artistic flair. The tasting menu, which may feature items like Arctic char with Labrador tea or venison tartare with pickled spruce tips, offers a truly immersive food experience.

3. Le Clocher Penché

Type: French Bistro | Local & Seasonal
Address: 203 Rue Saint-Joseph Est, Québec City, QC G1K 3B1
Contact: +1 418-640-0597
Website: www.clocherpenche.ca
Price Range: $$

Key Features:

- Housed in a former presbytery with a charming, relaxed atmosphere
- Known for brunch and lunch as much as for dinner
- Wine list emphasizing biodynamic and local producers

Overview:

A Saint-Roch district staple, Le Clocher Penché offers inspired cuisine in a casual setting. With plates that change regularly, you might find dishes such as duck confit with caramelized onions or poached eggs with pancetta and hollandaise. It's especially popular with locals for weekend brunch.

4. Le Lapin Sauté

Type: Traditional Québécois | Bistro
Address: 52 Rue du Petit-Champlain, Québec City, QC G1K 4H4
Contact: +1 418-692-5325
Website: www.lapinsaute.com
Price Range: $$

Key Features:

- Cozy bistro specializing in rabbit and duck dishes
- Nestled in the heart of the Petit-Champlain district
- Rustic decor with floral-filled terrace in summer

Overview:

Le Lapin Sauté is a quintessential Québécois dining experience, with a menu centered on slow-cooked comfort foods. Try the rabbit cassoulet or duck confit salad, paired with a local cider or Quebec wine. The friendly, informal service and location on one of the prettiest streets in North America add to its charm.

5. La Planque

Type: Upscale Contemporary | Gastro-Pub
Address: 1027 3e Avenue, Québec City, QC G1L 2X3
Contact: +1 418-914-8780
Website: www.laplanquerestaurant.com
Price Range: $$$

Key Features:

- Inventive dishes in a hip, hidden-away Limoilou location
- Emphasis on seafood and locally foraged items
- Stylish open-concept kitchen

Overview:
La Planque marries fine dining with a laid-back pub vibe. The chef's creativity is evident in dishes like wild mushroom risotto with spruce oil or seared scallops with dashi. It's a go-to spot for foodies seeking upscale innovation without the formality.

6. Bistro Hortus

Type: Sustainable Dining | Urban Garden Cuisine
Address: 1190 Rue Saint-Jean, Québec City, QC G1R 1S6
Contact: +1 418-692-0030
Website: www.bistrohortus.com
Price Range: $$

Key Features:

- Uses produce grown on the restaurant's rooftop garden
- Certified sustainable meat and seafood
- Eco-conscious atmosphere and decor

Overview:
Bistro Hortus offers fresh, vibrant meals focused on health and sustainability. The garden-to-table menu changes frequently and features options like beet tartare, bison burgers, and seafood chowder. The commitment to environmental responsibility is visible in everything from sourcing to plating.

7. L'Affaire est Ketchup

Type: Contemporary Quebecois | Casual Fine Dining
Address: 46 Rue Saint-Joseph Est, Québec City, QC G1K 3A5

Contact: +1 418-529-9020
Website: N/A (Reservations by phone or walk-in)
Price Range: $$–$$$

Key Features:

- Wildly creative and unpretentious
- Tiny dining room, kitchen in plain view
- Funky decor with a no-rules attitude

Overview:
 With no printed menu and an ever-changing blackboard list of seasonal creations, L'Affaire est Ketchup is an experience as much as it is a meal. Expect bold combinations like blood sausage with apple compote or char with beet purée and smoked butter. Reservations are essential, as the restaurant is small and in high demand.

8. Nina Pizza Napolitaine

Type: Casual | Neapolitan Pizza
Address: 410 Rue Saint-Anselme, Québec City, QC G1K 5T2
Contact: +1 418-255-1234
Website: www.ninapizza.ca
Price Range: $–$$

Key Features:

- Authentic wood-fired pizza
- Simple menu with fresh ingredients
- Urban ambiance in Saint-Roch district

Overview:
 For a break from French-heavy fare, Nina Pizza offers top-tier Neapolitan pizza with chewy crusts and vibrant toppings. Popular with both locals and visitors, it's ideal for a casual lunch or relaxed dinner without sacrificing quality.

5.3 Best Cafés, Bistros & Bakeries

Québec City's café and bakery scene is a delightful reflection of its French heritage, local creativity, and slow-living charm. Whether you're in search of the perfect buttery croissant, a cozy café tucked into a cobblestone alley, or a neighborhood bistro with comforting fare, the city offers an abundance of warm, character-filled spots to sip, savor, and unwind.

From **classic patisseries to trendy third-wave coffee shops**, this curated selection highlights some of the best places to pause and enjoy the tastes of Québec.

Cafés: Artisanal Coffee & Cozy Corners

Café Saint-Henri

- **Location:** 849 Rue Saint-Joseph Est, Saint-Roch
- **Specialties:** Espresso drinks, Chemex pour-over, locally roasted beans
- **Vibe:** Minimalist, modern, with large windows and community tables
- **Why Visit:** A leading name in Québec's specialty coffee scene, Café Saint-Henri roasts its beans locally and prides itself on transparency and traceability.

Cantook Micro Torréfaction

- **Location:** 575 Rue Saint-Jean, Old Québec
- **Specialties:** Micro-roasted coffee, flat white, cold brew
- **Vibe:** Intimate and rustic with a wooden interior and indie playlists
- **Why Visit:** This tiny, aromatic space is serious about its craft. Baristas are friendly, and beans can be bought to go.

Maelstrøm Saint-Roch

- **Location:** 181 Rue Saint-Vallier Est
- **Specialties:** Nitro cold brew, brunch-style bites, inventive lattes
- **Vibe:** Eclectic and hip, with a laid-back local crowd
- **Why Visit:** Part café, part cocktail bar. Great for remote work in the morning or creative cocktails in the evening.

Café Félin Ma Langue Aux Chats

- **Location:** 757 Rue Saint-Jean
- **Specialties:** Lattes, teas, pastries
- **Vibe:** Cat café with a mission—quiet, playful, and feline-friendly
- **Why Visit:** Enjoy a coffee while mingling with adoptable cats. Ideal for animal lovers and solo travelers.

Bakeries (Boulangeries & Pâtisseries): Flaky, Buttery Perfection

Paillard

- **Location:** 1097 Rue Saint-Jean, Old Québec
- **Specialties:** Croissants, macarons, tarte au sucre, baguette sandwiches
- **Why Visit:** This bustling boulangerie is a must for pastry lovers. Their croissants are among the best in the city—airy, golden, and just sweet enough.

Le Croquembouche

- **Location:** 225 Rue Saint-Joseph Est, Saint-Roch
- **Specialties:** Éclairs, canelés, artisan bread, custom cakes
- **Why Visit:** A feast for the eyes and the palate. Their pastry cases look like edible art exhibits. Don't miss the praline cream puffs.

Boulangerie Pâtisserie Simon

- **Location:** 158 Rue Racine, Limoilou
- **Specialties:** Multigrain loaves, kouign-amann, quiches
- **Why Visit:** A community staple that combines artisanal bread with authentic French pastries. Great for a takeaway breakfast.

La Boîte à Pain

- **Location:** 289 Rue Saint-Joseph Est (multiple locations)
- **Specialties:** Organic breads, fougasses, butter tarts

- **Why Visit:** Known for their handmade, hearty loaves and generous baked goods. A solid choice for vegetarians.

Bistros: Local Charm, Seasonal Fare & Casual Elegance

Bistro L'Accent

- **Location:** 880 Rue Honoré-Mercier
- **Menu Highlights:** Duck confit salad, onion soup, Québec cheeses
- **Vibe:** Intimate with rustic wood interiors and a loyal local crowd
- **Why Visit:** A go-to for lunch with flair—elegant but unpretentious, focused on local ingredients.

Bistro Hortus

- **Location:** 1190 Rue Saint-Jean
- **Menu Highlights:** Wild mushroom risotto, Québec lamb, seasonal cocktails
- **Vibe:** Bright and contemporary with rooftop beehives and herbs
- **Why Visit:** A sustainable bistro where ingredients come from their own rooftop garden or nearby farms.

Buvette Scott

- **Location:** 821 Rue Scott, Saint-Jean-Baptiste
- **Menu Highlights:** Small plates, natural wines, fresh pasta
- **Vibe:** Trendy and compact, with an ever-changing blackboard menu
- **Why Visit:** One of Québec City's best-kept secrets for foodies. Known for its rotating wine list and excellent sharing plates.

Traveler Tips for Enjoying the City's Café Culture

- **Order Etiquette:** When in doubt, greet with "Bonjour!" and wait to be seated at bistros. In cafés, ordering at the counter is typical.
- **Takeout Culture:** Common and encouraged, especially at bakeries. Perfect for a picnic near the Old Port or the Plains of Abraham.
- **Opening Hours:** Many cafés open around 8–9 AM and close by 4–6 PM. Bistros often open for lunch and re-open in the evening around 5–6 PM.
- **Local Favorites:** Try regional specialties like **tarte au sucre**, **croissant aux amandes**, or a café au lait avec **maple syrup** stirred in.

From flakey pastries in the morning sun to evening wine and shared plates in a cozy corner bistro, Québec City offers the perfect culinary pause between your explorations.

These spots aren't just about eating—they're about savoring the city's soul, one bite and one sip at a time.

Chapter 6. Festivals & Events

6.1 Winter Carnival (Carnaval de Québec)

"The cold never stopped us — it made us celebrate harder."

Québec City's **Winter Carnival**, known locally as *Carnaval de Québec*, is the crown jewel of the city's cultural calendar and one of the most iconic winter festivals in the world. First held in 1894 and revived in its modern form in 1955, this annual celebration transforms the city into a lively, snow-covered wonderland where Quebecers embrace the season with music, parades, sports, and spirited traditions that warm even the chilliest nights.

Overview

- **When:** Late January to mid-February (varies by year)
- **Where:** Various locations across Québec City — major sites include the Plains of Abraham, Old Quebec, and Place d'Youville
- **Typical Duration:** ~2 weeks

- **Website:** www.carnaval.qc.ca

The Winter Carnival is one of the **largest and oldest winter festivals** in the world, attracting **hundreds of thousands of visitors** each year. Its slogan *"Bonhomme Carnaval vous souhaite la bienvenue!"* (Bonhomme welcomes you!) is familiar to anyone who's attended.

Key Features & Events

Bonhomme Carnaval: The Living Mascot

The heart and soul of the Carnival is **Bonhomme**, a cheerful snowman dressed in a red tuque and ceinture fléchée (traditional arrow sash). Far more than a mascot, Bonhomme is the official "mayor" of the festival — he even has a castle built for him every year.

- **Meet & Greet Bonhomme:** Take photos with him at events or in his Ice Palace.
- **Bonhomme's Ice Palace:** A stunning structure of ice and lights, located near the Plains of Abraham, open for public visits and nighttime illuminations.

Night Parades

Held on two weekends in different parts of the city (Upper and Lower Town), these evening spectacles feature:

- Floats, fire-breathers, dancers, and acrobats
- Themed performances and marching bands
- Bonhomme leading the parade in his royal sleigh
- Crowds bundled in parkas, lining snow-covered streets under the glow of winter lights

Snow Sculpting Competitions

Held on the Plains of Abraham, artists from across Québec and around the world compete to create towering sculptures from snow. Wander among the masterpieces and vote for your favorite.

- **Categories:** National and international
- **Lighting:** At night, the sculptures are beautifully illuminated

Ice Canoe Races

A uniquely Québecois sport, this thrilling race on the partially frozen St. Lawrence River sees teams of paddlers push canoes across treacherous ice floes and through frigid waters.

- **Location:** Bassin Louise, near the Old Port
- **When:** Usually the second weekend of the Carnival
- **Experience Level:** Extreme! But watching is half the fun.

Outdoor Dance Parties & Live Music

The Carnival hosts a range of open-air concerts and DJ sets — from folk to electronic — with heated tents and fire pits available.

- **Venues:** Place George-V, Place d'Youville, and smaller neighborhood hubs
- **Bonhomme's Ball:** A classic celebration of music, masks, and dancing

Traditional Activities

- **Maple taffy on snow** (*tire d'érable*) — a must-try treat!
- **Snow slides** and **giant ice slides** for kids and adults
- **Horse-drawn sleigh rides** through Old Quebec
- **Dog sledding and axe throwing** at select sites
- **Caribou drink** — a warm, fortified local beverage served in ice glasses

Visitor Services

- **Effigy Pass:** A small Bonhomme-shaped pass (usually ~$20 CAD) gives you access to most paid sites and events for the entire festival.
- **Family Zones:** Dedicated areas for kids with games, mascots, and indoor rest zones.
- **Food Vendors:** Poutine, beaver tails, maple treats, hot chocolate, and warm mulled wine abound throughout the city.
- **Warm-up Chalets:** Heated tents and rest stops are available at major venues.
- **Accessibility:** Key sites are accessible for those with reduced mobility.

What to Wear

Québec winters are notoriously cold — temperatures often dip below −20°C (−4°F). To enjoy the Carnival comfortably:

- **Layer up** with thermal base layers, wool sweaters, and windproof outerwear

- Wear **insulated boots, hats, gloves, and scarves**
- Hand and foot warmers are commonly sold on-site
- Most Carnival-goers sport a **ceinture fléchée (sash)** — available for purchase at festival shops

The Spirit of Carnival

The Winter Carnival is more than just a festival — it's a cultural phenomenon that embodies the Quebecois attitude toward winter: don't hide from it, celebrate it. Locals and tourists gather regardless of wind or snow to share warmth, music, laughter, and a shot of Caribou in a glass made of ice.

Bonhomme Carnaval isn't just a mascot — he's a symbol of joy, resilience, and Quebec's love for life, even when it's below freezing.

6.2 Summer Festivals & Outdoor Shows

While Québec City is famous for its winter charm, summer brings an equally dynamic energy. As the snow melts and the streets fill with color, locals and visitors flock to a full calendar of festivals that take advantage of the city's stunning outdoor venues, historic architecture, and natural surroundings. From international music festivals to immersive cultural showcases, Québec City's summer season is a celebration of creativity, community, and joie de vivre.

Below is an in-depth look at the most prominent summer festivals and open-air events in the city.

Festival d'été de Québec (FEQ)

Type: International Music Festival
When: Early to mid-July (10–11 days)
Where: Plains of Abraham, Place d'Youville, and various stages across the city
Website: www.feq.ca

Overview:
Québec City's **Festival d'été** is one of the largest and most respected music festivals in Canada. It attracts global superstars and rising talents across multiple genres — from rock, pop, and hip-hop to indie, folk, and classical.

Notable Features:

- **Main Stage on the Plains of Abraham**: A historic battlefield turned into an electrifying concert venue for 80,000+ fans.
- **Place d'Youville & Parc de la Francophonie**: More intimate settings featuring francophone artists, experimental acts, and local performers.
- **Passes**: Affordable all-access wristbands (~$130–$150 CAD for 11 days) make this one of the best-valued major festivals in North America.

Past Artists: The Rolling Stones, Lady Gaga, Kendrick Lamar, Foo Fighters, Alanis Morissette, Imagine Dragons, Florence + the Machine, and more.

Grands Feux Loto-Québec (The Great Fireworks Show)

Type: Pyromusical Fireworks & Entertainment
When: August, twice a week (typically Thursdays and Sundays)
Where: Launched from the St. Lawrence River; visible from Old Port, Château Frontenac boardwalk, Lévis waterfront
Website: www.lesgrandsfeux.com

Overview:
These dazzling fireworks displays are choreographed to music and themes, lighting up the skies over the river with brilliant color. Spectators gather on both sides of the river for a shared celebration beneath the stars.

Features:

- Each night has a **unique theme**, such as jazz, cinema, or cultural fusion
- **Free and family-friendly**
- Live performances, DJs, and food trucks set up at prime viewing areas
- Bring a blanket or lawn chair for best viewing from the Dufferin Terrace or Old Port

New France Festival (Fêtes de la Nouvelle-France)

Type: Historical & Cultural Celebration
When: Early August (typically 5 days)
Where: Old Quebec (Upper and Lower Town)
Website: www.nouvellefrance.qc.ca

Overview:
Step back in time to the 17th and 18th centuries during the **Fêtes de la Nouvelle-France**, a lively celebration of Québec's colonial heritage. Streets are transformed with costumed performers, parades, and re-enactments.

Key Highlights:

- Street theater, folk dancing, and traditional music
- Historical encampments and artisan craft demonstrations
- Guided tours, lectures, and family-friendly workshops
- Locals and tourists alike wear **period costumes** to enhance the experience

ComédiHa! Fest-Québec

Type: Comedy & Performing Arts Festival
When: August (dates vary)
Where: Grand Théâtre de Québec, Agora Port de Québec, Place d'Youville
Website: www.comediha.com

Overview:
This laugh-out-loud festival brings together comedians from Québec, across Canada, and around the world. With a mix of outdoor stages and ticketed indoor performances, it's a lively, accessible way to enjoy Québec's famous sense of humor.

Features:

- Stand-up comedy in French and English
- Improv battles, sketch shows, and street performances

- Free shows in central squares and parks
- Rising stars and household names share the stage

Festibière de Québec (Québec City Beer Festival)

Type: Craft Beer & Food Festival
When: Mid to late August
Where: Old Port (Espace Quatre Cents)
Website: www.festibiere.ca

Overview:

This open-air festival is a paradise for beer lovers. Featuring over 75 breweries and hundreds of craft beer options, it also includes cider, spirits, and gourmet food trucks.

Highlights:

- **Tasting passport system** for samples
- Local bands and DJs throughout the day
- **Beer education workshops** and meet-the-brewer events
- Craft tents, picnic zones, and family areas with games

Passages Insolites (Unusual Passages)

Type: Public Art & Urban Exploration
When: Summer to early fall (June to October)
Where: Spread across Old Québec and Saint-Roch
Website: www.passagesinsolites.com

Overview:

More of an art circuit than a traditional festival, **Passages Insolites** showcases bold, interactive installations by local and international artists. The works are scattered through historic streets, alleyways, and parks, inviting spontaneous discovery and reflection.

Features:

- Guided and self-guided walking tours
- Contemporary sculpture, conceptual art, and site-specific designs
- Family-friendly and completely free
- Ideal for photography and cultural immersion

Free Outdoor Shows & Street Performances

All summer long, the streets of Québec City come alive with free performances—especially in tourist areas like Place Royale, Rue du Petit-Champlain, and the Dufferin Terrace. The city often schedules:

- Outdoor classical concerts by the **Orchestre symphonique de Québec**
- Impromptu **busker shows**, magicians, and musicians
- Free summer movies projected in the parks
- Pop-up **circus acts** by Cirque Éloize or local performers

These informal events contribute to the city's festive summer mood, blurring the line between planned celebration and joyful spontaneity.

6.3 Cultural & Art Events

Québec City is more than a picturesque destination—it's a cultural powerhouse. Rooted in French-Canadian heritage and shaped by a thriving artistic community, the city hosts a wide variety of events year-round that celebrate literature, visual arts, performance, and multicultural expression. These festivals and exhibitions reflect both Québec's historic identity and its evolving creative pulse, inviting residents and visitors to explore art in galleries, public spaces, and performance halls across the city.

Below are the most significant cultural and art-focused events in Québec City, each adding its own color to the city's vibrant cultural landscape.

Manif d'art – Québec City Biennial

Type: Contemporary Art Biennial
When: Every two years (late winter to spring; next edition in 2026)
Where: Multiple indoor and outdoor venues, including MNBAQ and public spaces
Website: www.manifdart.org

Overview:

Québec City's premier contemporary art event, the **Manif d'art Biennial**, transforms the city into a massive canvas for emerging and established artists. The festival blends gallery installations with outdoor interventions, thought-provoking visual art, and experimental media, all curated under a central theme.

Key Features:

- Multidisciplinary works: sculpture, video, installations, digital art
- Exhibits in museums, libraries, storefronts, and unexpected urban corners
- Family-friendly workshops and guided tours
- Showcases both Québec artists and international talents

Carrefour international de théâtre

Type: International Theater Festival
When: Late May to early June
Where: Grand Théâtre de Québec, La Bordée, Théâtre Périscope, and outdoor locations
Website: www.carrefourtheatre.qc.ca

Overview:

This internationally recognized theater festival presents daring, imaginative productions that span the boundaries of classical and contemporary performance. The **"Où tu vas quand tu dors en marchant?"** (Where Do You Go When You Sleepwalk?) The series is a signature open-air theatrical experience, with immersive nighttime performances staged across urban landscapes.

Highlights:

- French-language and international performances (some with English subtitles)
- Open-air interactive theater installations throughout the city
- Bold programming that includes puppetry, dance, and street theater

- Unique engagement with architecture, urban space, and audience movement

Québec BD (Festival de la bande dessinée francophone)

Type: Francophone Comic Art & Graphic Novel Festival
When: April
Where: Musée de la civilisation and other downtown venues
Website: www.quebecbd.com

Overview:
Québec BD celebrates the rich world of comic books, graphic novels, and sequential art with a Francophone focus. It brings together illustrators, writers, publishers, and fans through exhibitions, author meet-and-greets, book signings, and creative workshops.

Features:

- Artist alley and publishing showcases
- Original art exhibitions and sketch battles
- Workshops for all ages, including youth programs
- Focus on Québec, European, and international comic styles

Festival de cinéma de la ville de Québec (FCVQ)

Type: International Film Festival
When: September
Where: Théâtre Capitole, Cinéma Le Clap, Musée de la civilisation
Website: www.fcvq.ca

Overview:
This week-long festival brings global and Québécois cinema to the forefront, offering curated selections of narrative films, documentaries, shorts, and experimental works. The FCVQ celebrates both established filmmakers and emerging voices.

Key Features:

- Québec premieres and global retrospectives
- Outdoor screenings in public squares
- Audience Q&A sessions and panel discussions
- Industry events and awards for local and international films

Symposium International d'Art Contemporain de Baie-Saint-Paul

Type: Live Art Creation & Exhibition (day trip-worthy event)
When: July to August
Where: Baie-Saint-Paul (1 hour 30 minutes from Québec City)
Website: www.symposiumbaiesaintpaul.com

Overview:
Though located just outside Québec City, this symposium is worth the detour. Artists from around the world create work live before audiences over the span of a month, offering a rare glimpse into the process of contemporary art-making in real time.

Highlights:

- Public engagement with artists
- On-site art sales and exhibitions
- Focus on innovation and experimentation
- Strong ties to the region's historical support for the arts (Baie-Saint-Paul is where Cirque du Soleil began)

Ex Muro – Urban Art Festival

Type: Street Art & Public Mural Festival
When: Late summer to early fall
Where: Saint-Roch and Saint-Sauveur districts
Website: www.exmuro.com

Overview:
This festival turns overlooked urban spaces into dynamic art experiences through bold murals, installations, and street performances. It celebrates public art as a living, breathing part of the city.

Key Features:

- Large-scale murals created live on city walls
- Local and international street artists
- Pop-up exhibitions and performances
- Free urban art walking tours and guided discovery routes

Musée de la civilisation – Rotating Exhibitions & Cultural Programming

Type: Year-Round Museum Programming
Where: 85 Rue Dalhousie, Québec City, QC G1K 7A6
Website: www.mcq.org

Overview:
While not a festival per se, the Musée de la civilisation is a cornerstone of the city's cultural fabric, with exhibitions that often mirror current social, historical, and artistic dialogues in Québec and beyond.

Highlights:

- Major themed exhibits on Indigenous culture, science, fashion, and world heritage
- Temporary exhibits tied to city-wide festivals
- Hands-on workshops and educational events for families
- Multimedia art installations and traveling international exhibits

From open-air theater under the stars to avant-garde gallery installations and immersive city-wide art walks, Québec City's cultural scene reflects a rich blend of tradition and cutting-edge experimentation. Whether you're a devoted art lover or a curious explorer, these festivals and events offer year-round opportunities to engage with the spirit of creativity that defines the city.

6.4 Holiday Markets & Seasonal Celebrations

Winter in Québec City is not just about snow and cold—it's a season of wonder, warmth, and tradition. When December approaches, the city transforms into a glowing winter village, complete with cobblestone streets wrapped in lights, pine garlands hung over 17th-century doorways, and markets echoing with carols and the scent of roasted chestnuts. Québec City's holiday atmosphere is often compared to the classic European Christmas towns of Germany, Austria, or Alsace—only here, it comes with a Québécois twist.

This magical time is filled with festive markets, illuminated streets, and joyful celebrations that stretch from late November into the New Year.

German Christmas Market (Marché de Noël Allemand de Québec)

When: Late November to late December
Where: Place de l'Hôtel-de-Ville and surrounding squares in Old Québec
Website: www.noelallemandquebec.com

Overview:
This award-winning market brings authentic Old World charm to the heart of Old Québec. Modeled after traditional European holiday markets, it features over 90 charming wooden kiosks selling German crafts, Québécois artisan gifts, and warm

seasonal delicacies. The market spans several squares, creating a festive trail beneath twinkling lights and a glowing Christmas tree.

Key Features:

- Handmade crafts, ornaments, woolen goods, wood carvings, candles
- Traditional food and drinks including bratwurst, gingerbread, mulled wine (*Glühwein*), and maple treats
- Live brass bands, choirs, folk performances, and costumed characters
- Family zones with puppet shows, storytelling, and Santa Claus visits
- Warm-up zones and heated terraces

Visitor Services:

- Open-air, free admission
- Wheelchair accessible and stroller-friendly
- Rest areas with heating lamps
- Multilingual signage (French, English, German)

Old Québec's Holiday Lights & Décorations (Décembre en Ville)

When: Late November to early January
Where: Throughout Old Québec, including Rue du Petit-Champlain, Dufferin Terrace, and Place Royale
Website: www.quebecregion.com

Overview:

Even outside the markets, Old Québec glows with the warmth of the holidays. Every street and square is draped in lights, wreaths, ribbons, and glowing lanterns. Horse-drawn carriages glide past storefronts glowing with festive decor, while Christmas music fills the air from speakers tucked into alleyways and plazas.

Highlights:

- **Rue du Petit-Champlain:** Often considered one of the most beautifully decorated streets in North America during the holidays
- **Place Royale:** Home to a massive, decorated tree surrounded by historic stone buildings
- **Dufferin Terrace:** Overlooks the icy St. Lawrence River with stunning photo ops at twilight

Salon des Artisans de Québec

When: Early to mid-December
Where: Centre de foires ExpoCité
Website: www.salondesartisansdequebec.com

Overview:

This massive indoor fair showcases the work of over 250 local artisans and designers. It's the perfect place to find unique gifts, gourmet food items, art, and winter fashion—directly from the makers.

Key Features:

- Jewelry, textiles, glassware, ceramics, holiday decor
- Local food specialties: maple syrups, jams, cheeses, charcuterie
- Cooking demos, live workshops, and music
- Shuttle buses run from downtown during peak hours

Le Grand Marché de Noël (Christmas at the Grand Marché de Québec)

When: December
Where: Le Grand Marché de Québec, 250-M Boulevard Wilfrid-Hamel
Website: www.legrandmarchedequebec.com

Overview:
A modern covered marketplace infused with rustic holiday charm. The Grand Marché dresses up for the season with lights, trees, music, and a full calendar of festive events. It's a great destination for fresh seasonal produce, gourmet food, and culinary gifts.

Features:

- Indoor Christmas village with artisan booths
- Tastings of local cider, wine, cheese, and preserves
- Kids' workshops, cooking demos, and Santa Claus visits
- On-site bakeries and chocolatiers offering holiday treats

Midnight Mass at Notre-Dame de Québec Basilica-Cathedral

When: December 24, Midnight
Where: 16 Rue De Buade, Québec City, QC G1R 4A1
Website: www.ndq.qc.ca

Overview:
The midnight Christmas Eve Mass at this UNESCO-listed basilica is one of the most spiritually and culturally significant events of the holiday season. The cathedral's interior glows with candles and stained glass, and the choir performs a moving repertoire of traditional Christmas hymns.

Visitor Notes:

- Doors open early due to high attendance
- Open to all, regardless of faith tradition
- French-language service, with some English guidance
- Suggested attire: formal or respectful winterwear

New Year's Eve Celebrations on Grande Allée

When: December 31
Where: Grande Allée & Place de l'Assemblée-Nationale
Website: www.quebecregion.com

Overview:

Ring in the New Year with one of the most spirited outdoor parties in the province. Grande Allée becomes a festive corridor of open-air dance floors, street performers, light shows, and music stages. At midnight, fireworks explode above the city skyline, accompanied by a countdown celebration seen and heard throughout the area.

Key Features:

- Free outdoor concerts by Québec artists
- Light shows and projections on government buildings
- Food stalls, hot chocolate stands, bars, and patios
- Family-friendly areas earlier in the evening; lively crowds closer to midnight

Tips for Visitors:

- Dress warmly in multiple layers—temps often drop well below freezing
- Public transportation runs extended hours
- Expect crowds: arrive early for a good viewing spot

Practical Tips for Holiday Visitors

- **Book accommodations early** (especially around Christmas and New Year) — Old Québec hotels fill up fast.
- **Layer your clothing** — It's not uncommon for temperatures to fall below −20°C (−4°F).
- **Look out for pop-up choirs** and spontaneous caroling on Rue Saint-Jean and at Place d'Youville.
- **Take advantage of the city's winter shuttle buses,** which often operate during holiday events.
- **Visit the Château Frontenac,** even if only to admire the stunning holiday decor and towering lobby tree.

Québec City during the holidays is the embodiment of winter magic — where every window flickers with warmth, every square hums with joy, and snowflakes fall like confetti on a city that truly knows how to celebrate the season.

Chapter 7. Outdoor Activities & Day Trips

7.1 Cycling & Riverfront Trails

Québec City is a cyclist's dream for both casual riders and more seasoned adventurers. With a mix of urban bike paths, forested routes, historic corridors, and scenic riverside trails, cycling is not just a mode of transport—it's a rewarding way to explore the natural beauty and cultural richness of the region.

Thanks to investments in safe, interconnected paths and a supportive cycling culture, visitors can enjoy everything from leisurely rides along the St. Lawrence River to ambitious day trips into the countryside.

Route Verte Network

Overview:
Québec's province-wide **Route Verte** is one of the most comprehensive cycling trail

systems in North America. In and around Québec City, it offers seamless access to riverfront paths, bridges, parks, and nearby towns.

- **Marked, paved trails** with minimal vehicle traffic
- **Rest stops, picnic areas, and lookouts** along the way
- Part of the national Trans Canada Trail (Great Trail)

Corridor du Littoral (Waterfront Corridor Trail)

Distance: ~50 km (31 mi)
Difficulty: Easy to moderate
Type: Paved, multi-use path
Start/End: From Montmorency Falls to Saint-Augustin-de-Desmaures

Overview:
This flagship cycling route runs along the **north shore of the St. Lawrence River**, offering spectacular water views and access to multiple key sites. It's perfect for families, casual cyclists, and long-distance riders.

Highlights:

- **Old Port and Vieux-Québec:** Cobblestone alleys and waterfront cafés
- **Battles of the Plains of Abraham site:** A historic park with picnic spots
- **Samuel-De Champlain Promenade:** A modern, beautifully landscaped trail with lookouts, art installations, and beach access
- **Cap-Rouge Marina:** Ideal for a scenic break or coffee
- Connects with inland green spaces and small villages for further exploration

Visitor Tips:

- Several **bike rental kiosks** are located along the trail
- **Public restrooms** and **drinking fountains** available seasonally
- Ideal for photography and birdwatching

Vélopiste Jacques-Cartier/Portneuf Trail

Distance: ~68 km (42 mi)
Difficulty: Easy to moderate
Type: Crushed-stone trail (suitable for hybrids/mountain bikes)
Start/End: Saint-Gabriel-de-Valcartier to Rivière-à-Pierre

Overview:
This scenic, countryside rail-trail runs through **forests, lakes, farmlands**, and

charming rural towns northwest of Québec City. It's well-loved by nature lovers and is a great choice for a peaceful escape from the urban core.

Highlights:

- **Old train stations converted into rest areas**
- **Interpretive signs** on history, flora, and fauna
- Nearby camping and B&B options for multi-day rides
- **Wildlife viewing**: foxes, herons, beavers, and seasonal butterflies

Île d'Orléans Loop

Distance: ~67 km (41 mi) full loop
Difficulty: Intermediate (due to hills and narrow roads)
Type: On-road cycling with paved shoulders
Start/End: Bridge access via Route 368 from Beauport

Overview:

Often described as a step back in time, **Île d'Orléans** is a pastoral island just 15 minutes from downtown Québec City. The full loop circles farms, orchards, vineyards, historic homes, and stunning river views.

Key Stops Along the Loop:

- **Cider and wine producers**: Tastings available at places like Domaine Steinbach
- **Fromageries** and strawberry farms (seasonal)
- **18th-century churches and rural hamlets**
- **Lookouts and picnic areas** with panoramic views of Mont-Sainte-Anne and the Laurentians

Important Notes:

- The road is shared with vehicles and can be narrow in spots
- Cyclists should have **experience with road riding and elevation changes**
- Allow 4–6 hours for the full loop, with time for stops

Montmorency Falls & Corridor de la Rivière Montmorency

Distance: ~10–15 km roundtrip
Difficulty: Easy
Type: Paved path and wooden walkways
Access Point: Parking area near Parc de la Chute-Montmorency

Overview:

A rewarding short ride that ends at one of Québec's most iconic natural sites: the 83-meter (272 ft) **Montmorency Falls**, which is taller than Niagara Falls. Cyclists can explore the base of the falls and continue along the quiet **Corridor de la Rivière Montmorency**, a tranquil path through nature.

Features:

- Bike racks and restrooms available at the falls
- Option to hike the **suspension bridge** or take the cable car (fee)
- Great for beginners or as a family-friendly half-day outing

Bike Rentals & Services

Cyclo Services

Location: 289 Rue Saint-Paul, Old Port
Website: www.cycloservices.net
Services: Bike rentals (city, hybrid, e-bike, tandem), guided bike tours, helmets, child trailers
Note: Open seasonally (May–October)

Location Echo Sports

Location: Near Promenade Samuel-De Champlain
Website: www.echosports.ca
Services: Performance and electric bike rentals, mountain and hybrid models, maps and repair tools

VéloVert – Québec's Public Bike Network (planned expansion by 2026)

Note: At present, Québec City does not have a full-scale bike-share program like Montréal's BIXI, but local initiatives and expanded bike lanes are in development under the **VéloVert** urban mobility strategy.

Practical Tips for Cyclists

- **Helmet use is highly recommended**, though not mandatory for adults in Québec
- Bring **cash or card** for roadside farm stands and cafés
- Summer weather is ideal (June to September), but **check forecasts for wind and rain** along riverfront trails

- Québec drivers are generally respectful, but **use proper hand signals and stay visible** when road riding
- Many trails are **multi-use**, so be mindful of pedestrians and inline skaters

From casual rides along the St. Lawrence to full-day island adventures and countryside escapes, Québec City's cycling culture is accessible, scenic, and deeply enriching. Whether you're pedaling past historic landmarks or picnicking beside a quiet river bend, there's no better way to discover the region's natural rhythm and beauty.

7.2 Skiing, Snowshoeing & Ice Activities

Québec City is not only one of North America's most picturesque winter cities—it's also a base for world-class snow sports and outdoor activities. From alpine ski slopes and backcountry trails to snowshoe routes, ice skating rinks, and thrilling toboggan runs, the region offers a winter playground for all skill levels and ages. Whether you're a seasoned skier, a first-time snowshoer, or simply seeking the joy of gliding across a frozen pond, Québec has you covered—sometimes literally in fresh powder.

Alpine Skiing & Snowboarding

Mont-Sainte-Anne

- **Location:** 40 km (25 mi) east of Québec City
- **Website:** www.mont-sainte-anne.com
- **Lift Tickets:** ~$70–$100 CAD (adult day pass)

Overview:
One of Eastern Canada's premier ski resorts, Mont-Sainte-Anne offers terrain for every level with **71 trails**, including **night skiing, freestyle parks**, and **unparalleled river views**. It boasts the **highest vertical drop for night skiing in Canada** and is known for early openings and late spring closures.

Key Features:

- Family zone and dedicated beginner lifts
- On-site rentals, ski school, and mountain restaurants
- Snowmaking across 80%+ of terrain
- Nordic center with snowshoe and cross-country trails nearby

Le Massif de Charlevoix

- **Location:** Petite-Rivière-Saint-François, 75 km (47 mi) from Québec City
- **Website:** www.lemassif.com
- **Lift Tickets:** ~$80–$105 CAD (adult day pass)

Overview:
With **the highest vertical drop east of the Rockies**, Le Massif is known for its **panoramic St. Lawrence River views**, deep powder, and terrain that challenges experienced skiers. It's also celebrated for its eco-conscious design and exceptional off-piste vibe.

Key Features:

- Backcountry-style glades and steep runs
- Modern gondolas and mountain-top lodge
- Heli-ski-style views over cliffs and frozen rivers
- Snowshoe trails, sledding experiences, and gourmet après-ski dining

Cross-Country Skiing (Ski de fond)

Base de plein air de Sainte-Foy

- **Location:** Sainte-Foy, 20 minutes from downtown
- **Trails:** ~30 km of groomed classic and skate skiing
- **Rental Available:** Yes

Sentiers du Camp Mercier (Réserve faunique des Laurentides)

- **Location:** ~1 hour north of the city
- **Website:** www.sepaq.com
- **Overview:** Top-tier groomed trails through Laurentian forests, ideal for intermediate to advanced skiers.

Features:

- Over 70 km of ski trails
- Heated shelters, waxing stations, and ski patrol
- Spectacular snowy landscapes and wildlife sightings

Snowshoeing Adventures

Parc national de la Jacques-Cartier

- **Location:** 40 km (25 mi) north of Québec City
- **Website:** www.sepaq.com/pq/jac
- **Rental Available:** Yes

Overview:
A pristine glacial valley filled with deep snow and dramatic scenery, this park offers over **11 marked snowshoe trails**, from easy river walks to ridge hikes with canyon views.

Highlights:

- Snowshoe-only zones for quiet immersion
- Interpretation panels and wildlife tracks
- Cozy winter cabins for overnight stays

Domaine Maizerets

- **Location:** Central Québec City

- **Overview:** An urban oasis with well-maintained paths, perfect for casual snowshoeing and nature walks. Free to access, rentals on-site.

Ice Skating Rinks in Québec City

Place d'Youville Rink

- **Location:** In front of Théâtre Capitole, near the Old City gates
- **Admission:** Free with own skates; rentals ~$10–15 CAD
- **Season:** Late November to March

Overview:
A postcard-perfect rink surrounded by Gothic and classical architecture, this rink is ideal for romantic glides and family fun. Open late with ambient music and lights.

Plains of Abraham Skating Trail (Anneau de Glace)

- **Location:** Battlefields Park
- **Overview:** A 500-meter skating loop along historic grounds, with warming huts, rentals, and hot chocolate nearby.

Village Nordik at Port de Québec

- **Location:** Bassin Louise, Old Port
- **Season:** Mid-winter (January–February)
- **Activities:** Ice skating, ice fishing, and giant snow slides
- **Website:** www.villagenordik.com

Iconic Tobogganing on Terrasse Dufferin

- **Location:** Beside Château Frontenac, Old Québec
- **Open:** Mid-December to March (weather permitting)
- **Cost:** ~$4 per ride or ~$12 for 4 rides
- **Rentals:** Toboggans available on-site

Overview:
This classic wooden toboggan run has thrilled locals and visitors since 1884. Riders fly downhill at speeds of up to 70 km/h with the majestic Château looming behind and the icy St. Lawrence River ahead.

Tips:

- Great for kids and adults

- Bundle up—wind chills are real on the ride down
- Best experienced in early evening with festive lighting

Winter Parks & Forest Escapes

Station Touristique Duchesnay

- **Location:** ~30 minutes west of the city
- **Activities:** Cross-country skiing, snowshoeing, tubing, dog sledding
- **Accommodations:** On-site lodge and cabins
- **Website:** www.sepaq.com/ct/duc

Centre de plein air de Beauport

- **Location:** East end of Québec City
- **Overview:** Accessible trails, sledding hills, and skating rinks—ideal for families or a quick winter outing close to the city.

Winter Equipment Rentals in the City

Québec Adventure Tours

- **Location:** Old Port
- **Rental Gear:** Skis, snowshoes, skates, sleds
- **Website:** www.quebecaventuretours.com

Patin Patin (Place d'Youville)

- **Services:** Skate rentals and sharpening
- **Open Hours:** Daily during rink season

SÉPAQ Parks & Duchesnay

- **On-site rentals:** Available for all snow equipment, with package deals for families and multi-day visitors

Practical Tips for Winter Activities

- **Dress in layers**: thermal base, insulating fleece, and waterproof outerwear
- **Footwear matters**: waterproof boots with grip are essential
- **Check weather and trail conditions** daily, especially for outdoor skating and mountain access
- **Sunlight is limited**: plan early starts and bring headlamps if venturing out late

- **Transportation**: Shuttle buses available to major resorts (especially on weekends); rental cars advised for rural trails

Whether you're carving downhill slopes with breathtaking views or snowshoeing through quiet forests where only your footsteps break the silence, Québec City offers unforgettable winter adventures in every direction. Embrace the cold, and you'll find warmth in the landscapes, traditions, and the joy of outdoor play.

7.3 Day Trips: Île d'Orléans, Wendake & Le Massif

Québec City is not just a destination—it's a gateway to some of the most culturally rich, scenic, and historic areas in the province. A short drive from the city can take you to a pastoral island rooted in colonial heritage, an Indigenous community preserving ancestral traditions, or one of Canada's most breathtaking ski mountains. These day trips offer refreshing contrasts to the urban core, while remaining easily accessible by car, shuttle, or guided tour.

Île d'Orléans: A Step Back in Time

- **Distance from Québec City:** 15 km (9 mi), ~20 minutes by car
- **Best For:** Countryside charm, local food & drink, cycling, heritage tours

- **Website:** www.iledorleans.com

Overview:

Known as "the cradle of French America," Île d'Orléans is a lush, agricultural island in the St. Lawrence River with a strong rural identity and a deep historical soul. The island's roads wind past ancestral homes, vineyards, orchards, and roadside stands that sell everything from strawberry jam to artisanal cheese. The entire island is a designated heritage site.

Top Experiences:

- **Wine & Cider Tasting:** Domaine Steinbach, Cassis Monna & Filles, and Vignoble Isle de Bacchus
- **Strawberry and Apple Picking:** Seasonal (June–October)
- **Cheese and Chocolates:** Visit Fromagerie Ferme Audet or Chocolaterie de l'Île
- **Sainte-Pétronille:** The island's western tip offers panoramic river views and boutiques
- **Maison Drouin (circa 1730):** One of the oldest preserved homes in Québec
- **Le Relais des Pins:** Traditional sugar shack meals (open in spring and select seasons)

Getting There:

- By car via the Île d'Orléans Bridge (Route 368)
- Guided tours available from Québec City (including wine & culinary routes)
- Ideal for **cycling the 67 km loop** (intermediate level)

Wendake: Living Huron-Wendat Culture

- **Distance from Québec City:** 17 km (11 mi), ~25 minutes by car
- **Best For:** Indigenous culture, heritage museums, traditional food, immersive experiences
- **Website:** www.tourismewendake.ca

Overview:

Wendake is the home of the Huron-Wendat Nation, one of the few places in Canada where visitors can experience living Indigenous culture. The community is known for preserving its language, rituals, arts, and ancestral knowledge while also embracing modern creativity.

Top Experiences:

- **Huron-Wendat Museum (Musée Huron-Wendat):** Learn about the nation's history, spirituality, and craftsmanship through exhibits and guided tours
- **Onhoua Chetek8e Traditional Site:** Explore a recreated longhouse village, watch dances and hear creation stories from Indigenous guides
- **Ekionkiestha' National Longhouse:** A striking ceremonial space that hosts storytelling nights and traditional feasts
- **Craft Shops & Galleries:** Handmade jewelry, leatherwork, and beadwork made by Huron artisans
- **Restaurant La Traite:** Fine Indigenous cuisine featuring game, wild berries, and native herbs

Visitor Services:

- Accessible by car, taxi, or organized day tours
- Hôtel-Musée Premières Nations offers immersive overnight stays in a boutique hotel infused with Indigenous design
- Events year-round including **powwows, artisan markets, and seasonal ceremonies**

Le Massif de Charlevoix: Nature & Adventure with a View

- **Distance from Québec City:** 75 km (47 mi), ~1 hour by car
- **Best For:** Alpine skiing, scenic drives, mountain biking, panoramic St. Lawrence views
- **Website:** www.lemassif.com

Overview:

Set along dramatic cliffs where the mountains drop into the St. Lawrence River, **Le Massif** offers both adrenaline-pumping sports and spectacular scenery. It boasts **the highest vertical drop east of the Rockies** and year-round activities that include winter skiing, summer hiking, and cultural events linked to the nearby Charlevoix region.

Winter Highlights:

- Skiing and snowboarding with deep natural snow and groomed trails
- Panoramic gondola rides with river and forest views
- Après-ski dining and spa services in the summit lodge

Summer Highlights:

- **Hiking & Mountain Biking:** Lift-serviced trails with epic river views
- **Railway Experience:** The Train de Charlevoix connects Québec City to Le Massif (seasonal)
- **Eco-lodging:** Unique accommodations including mountainside cabins and riverfront domes

Other Nearby Attractions (extend your day trip):

- **Baie-Saint-Paul:** An artistic hub with galleries, boutiques, and bistros
- **Charlevoix Flavour Trail:** Discover local producers of cheese, cider, chocolate, and craft beer

Getting There:

- Best reached by car; free parking at base and summit
- **Train de Charlevoix** (summer only): Scenic train ride from Québec City to Baie-Saint-Paul and Le Massif
- Bus shuttles offered during winter ski season

Quick Comparison Table

Destination	Travel Time	Best For	Season Highlights
Île d'Orléans	~20 min	Heritage, food, cycling, countryside charm	Spring–Fall (blossoms, harvest)
Wendake	~25 min	Indigenous culture, storytelling, cuisine	Year-round (museum & longhouse)
Le Massif	~1 hr	Skiing, hiking, mountain views	Winter (ski); Summer (bike & hike)

Whether you're sipping ice cider on an island farm, listening to ancestral stories inside a longhouse, or carving powder down a mountain ridge, these day trips offer deep connections to Québec's history, identity, and natural splendor—all within an easy escape from the city's center.

Chapter 8. Arts, History & Culture

8.1 Museums & Historic Sites

Québec City is a living museum. Its cobblestone streets, fortifications, and stone buildings carry the legacy of centuries, while its cultural institutions preserve, interpret, and celebrate the city's dynamic French-Canadian identity. From world-class museums and military fortresses to religious landmarks and interpretive centers, visitors can trace Québec's complex history—from its Indigenous roots to colonial struggles, cultural evolution, and modern creativity.

Musée de la civilisation (Museum of Civilization)

- **Location:** 85 Rue Dalhousie, Old Port (Vieux-Port)
- **Website:** www.mcq.org
- **Admission:** ~$18 CAD (adult), free for children under 12
- **Opening Hours:** Tuesday–Sunday, 10 AM – 5 PM

Overview:
Québec's premier cultural museum combines **interactive exhibits**, **multimedia**

storytelling, and **cutting-edge design** to bring history, society, and human experience to life. It's not just about artifacts—it's about context, identity, and dialogue.

Must-See Exhibits:

- "This is Our Story" – Co-created with Indigenous communities to present Wendat, Innu, and other First Nations' perspectives
- "People of Québec...Then and Now" – A sweeping journey from early settlers to today's multicultural society
- Rotating international exhibitions on topics ranging from fashion to mythology to science

Visitor Services:

- Guided tours, multilingual panels (French & English)
- Café, boutique gift shop, kid-friendly exhibits
- Fully wheelchair accessible

Musée national des beaux-arts du Québec (MNBAQ)

- **Location:** 179 Grande Allée Ouest, on the Plains of Abraham
- **Website:** www.mnbaq.org
- **Admission:** ~$24 CAD (adult), free for under 18
- **Opening Hours:** Tuesday–Sunday, 10 AM – 5 PM (Wednesdays until 9 PM)

Overview:

Set in a stunning architectural complex that includes a modern glass pavilion and a former prison, the MNBAQ is Québec's principal art museum. It celebrates **Québécois artists from the 17th century to today**, while hosting major international exhibitions.

Collection Highlights:

- Works by **Jean-Paul Riopelle**, **Alfred Pellan**, **Marc-Aurèle Fortin**, and contemporary Indigenous artists
- Period rooms, photography, sculpture, and installations
- Outdoor sculpture garden and exhibitions on design & decorative arts

Visitor Services:

- On-site bistro with seasonal menus
- Art workshops and interactive family programs
- Free admission on the first Sunday of every month

Fortifications of Québec – Parks Canada National Historic Site

- **Location:** Across Old Québec, accessible from Rue St-Louis and Rue d'Auteuil
- **Website:** www.pc.gc.ca/fortifications
- **Admission:** Included with most Parks Canada site passes

Overview:
Québec City is the **only walled city north of Mexico**, and these 4.6 km of preserved **17th- to 19th-century fortifications** tell the story of a city shaped by war, empire, and strategic geography. Walking the walls offers panoramic views and a sense of the city's resilience.

Highlights:

- **Artillery Park & Dauphine Redoubt** – Historic barracks and military life displays
- **Ramparts Walk** – An elevated stroll above Old Québec
- Cannons, lookout towers, interpretive signs, and guided walks

Tips:

- Best explored in spring to fall (some sections close in winter)
- Wear sturdy shoes—stone pathways can be uneven
- Excellent photo ops over rooftops and the river

Plains of Abraham (Battlefields Park)

- **Location:** Bordering Old Québec along the Grande Allée
- **Website:** www.ccbn-nbc.gc.ca
- **Admission:** Free to explore; museum entry ~$10 CAD

Overview:
Site of the **famous 1759 battle between the French and British**, this urban park blends sweeping green spaces with military history and cultural programming. It is both a memorial and a beloved community green space.

Attractions:

- **The Plains of Abraham Museum:** Tells the story of the Seven Years' War and includes uniforms, weapons, and interactive exhibits
- **Martello Towers:** 19th-century British fortifications with seasonal access
- **Cross-country ski trails, concerts, and festivals** held throughout the year

Citadelle of Québec & Royal 22e Régiment Museum

- **Location:** Atop Cap Diamant, adjacent to Château Frontenac
- **Website:** www.lacitadelle.qc.ca
- **Admission:** ~$18 CAD (includes guided tour)
- **Hours:** Daily, 9 AM – 5 PM (varies by season)

Overview:

Still an active military garrison, the **Citadelle** is a star-shaped fortress offering commanding views of the St. Lawrence River. It houses the **Royal 22e Régiment**, Canada's only francophone regular force unit.

Experiences:

- Guided tours through the ramparts and barracks
- Museum exhibits on Canadian military history
- **Changing of the Guard ceremony** (late June to early September)
- Cannon-firing demonstration and ceremonial events

Morrin Centre

- **Location:** 44 Chaussée des Écossais, Old Québec
- **Website:** www.morrin.org
- **Admission:** ~$15 CAD (guided tour recommended)

Overview:

Originally a prison, then a college, now a cultural center and English-language library, the Morrin Centre is a **hidden gem** that tells a layered story of Anglophone history in Québec.

Key Features:

- Victorian library with wrought-iron balconies and antique woodwork
- Restored 19th-century jail cells
- Literary events, heritage tours, and cultural programming in English

Château Frontenac (Historic Interiors & Tours)

- **Location:** 1 Rue des Carrières, Old Québec
- **Website:** www.fairmont.com/frontenac-quebec
- **Tour Admission:** ~$18 CAD (self-guided or with costumed interpreter)

Overview:

More than a luxury hotel, **Château Frontenac** is a landmark of Québec identity and architectural splendor. Explore its grand halls, lavish décor, and exhibits on the heads of state and celebrities who've stayed there.

What to See:

- **Historic exhibits** in the lower corridors and interpretive panels throughout
- Photo-worthy interiors: spiral staircases, chandeliers, and ballrooms
- Optional dining at **Le Champlain Restaurant** for a fine culinary experience with a side of history

Other Noteworthy Historic Sites

- **Notre-Dame de Québec Basilica-Cathedral:** The oldest Catholic parish north of Mexico; free to enter, donations welcome
- **Séminaire de Québec:** Founded in 1663, still an active theological institution with a historic chapel and cloister
- **Maison Chevalier:** A restored merchant's house-turned-museum in Petit-Champlain, showing life in 18th-century Québec

Tips for Museum & Heritage Visits

- Many sites are bilingual (French & English), but guided tours offer **deeper interpretation**
- **Parks Canada Discovery Pass** may offer bundled access to national historic sites
- Museums like MNBAQ and MCQ offer **free admission days** (check schedules)
- Combine museums with walking tours to **layer historical context with on-the-ground experience**
- Plan for **2–3 hours per major museum**, especially with interactive or multimedia exhibits

Québec City's museums and historic sites are more than collections—they are living narratives that let you stand in the footprints of colonists, soldiers, artisans, and visionaries. Whether you're marveling at art, following the echoes of battle drums, or descending into stone prisons, every visit deepens your understanding of a city that's proud of its past—and actively shaping its cultural future.

8.2 Local Artists & Galleries

Québec City is not only a center of history and architecture—it's a thriving canvas for contemporary creativity. From Indigenous artisans and street painters to world-renowned sculptors and avant-garde visual artists, the city boasts a diverse, flourishing arts scene. This is a place where **tradition meets innovation**, and where a walk through an alley or into a quiet studio might uncover a new perspective on Québécois identity and global expression.

Whether you're a collector, a curious browser, or an admirer of visual storytelling, these galleries and creative spaces offer an intimate look at the vibrant artistic heartbeat of Québec City.

Quartier Petit Champlain: Open-Air Artistry

- **Location:** Lower Town, Old Québec
- **Best For:** Local boutiques, artisan studios, handmade crafts, seasonal art fairs

Overview:
 Wander through **narrow cobblestone streets** lined with colorful facades and you'll find **artisans' shops**, galleries, and studios offering everything from **handmade**

jewelry and leather goods to **oil paintings and sculpture**. Many artists display their work in open storefronts, and you can often meet the creators in person.

Notable Spots:

- **Galerie d'Art du Petit Champlain** – Contemporary Québec artists in oil, acrylic, and mixed media
- **Atelier La Pomme** – Boutique studio specializing in wood, ceramic, and textile-based decorative art
- **Sculpteur Flamand** – Specializing in handcrafted bronze and wood sculptures with Québec motifs

Seasonal Events:

- **Winter & Summer Artist Markets**
- **Live painting demonstrations** during the summer tourist season

Rue Saint-Paul Art District

- **Location:** Old Port (Vieux-Port)
- **Best For:** Art collectors, antique hunters, painting and fine art browsing

Overview:
Rue Saint-Paul is known as Québec City's **gallery row**, home to numerous art galleries that range from traditional to experimental. You'll find everything from **classic landscape paintings** to **bold abstract works**, often framed by the original stone architecture of this heritage neighborhood.

Key Galleries:

- **Galerie Le Chien d'Or** – Showcasing fine art in contemporary realism and Québec landscapes
- **Galerie Lacerte Art Contemporain** – Features emerging and mid-career contemporary artists with a focus on Québec talent
- **Galerie Perreault** – One of the city's oldest commercial galleries, renowned for its oil paintings and sculpture collections

Galerie d'art uNo

- **Location:** 211 Rue Saint-Jean
- **Website:** www.galerieuno.com
- **Specialty:** Urban and contemporary pop art, often with a humorous or provocative edge

Overview:

A favorite among younger collectors and modern art lovers, uNo represents a roster of **local and international artists** known for bold colors, graffiti-influenced styles, and commentary on society and culture.

Visitor Tips:

- Expect rotating exhibitions with interactive or multimedia pieces
- The staff are knowledgeable and open to discussing pieces and artist bios

Maison de la Littérature (House of Literature)

- **Location:** 40 Rue Saint-Stanislas, Old Québec
- **Website:** www.maisondelalitterature.qc.ca
- **Focus:** Visual-literary installations, word-based design, Québecois authors and illustrators

Overview:

More than a literary space, this beautifully restored neo-Gothic church is a multidisciplinary hub for **word-based visual art**, including book design, calligraphy, and experimental exhibits exploring the power of language.

Features:

- Artist residencies and reading installations
- Free exhibits showcasing visual narratives from Québec writers and illustrators
- Café and bookshop attached

Indigenous Arts & Craft Galleries

Wendake Community Workshops & Galleries

- **Location:** Wendake, ~25 minutes from Québec City
- **Best For:** Authentic Indigenous artworks, carvings, beadwork, dreamcatchers

Overview:

Wendake is a center for **Huron-Wendat craftsmanship**, where you can find meaningful works rooted in spirituality and tradition. Pieces often reflect natural materials—stone, bone, leather, and wood—combined with precise design and symbolic meaning.

Recommended Stops:

- **La Boutique Wendake** – Beaded jewelry, moccasins, sculptures, and drums

- **Maison Tsawenhohi** – Historic site often used for artist residencies and cultural exchange

Coopérative Méduse

- **Location:** 591 Rue De Saint-Vallier Est, Saint-Roch District
- **Website:** www.meduse.org
- **Focus:** Interdisciplinary, experimental, collaborative arts

Overview:
Méduse is a **multidisciplinary arts cooperative** unlike any other in the province. It houses **10 cultural organizations** under one roof, including **art galleries, media labs, studios, and performance venues**. This is the place to see cutting-edge installations, video art, and art/technology collaborations.

Key Spaces:

- **Vidéographe & Avatar** – Specializing in sound and digital media
- **VU Photo** – Photography-focused gallery with frequent artist talks
- **Engramme** – Center for printmaking and screen-print art

Visitor Experience:

- Open to the public; check their calendar for current exhibitions and art events
- Often hosts free workshops, lectures, and experimental art shows

Artists' Studios & Collectives

Atelier Paré (Woodcarving Folk Art)

- **Location:** Sainte-Anne-de-Beaupré (~40 minutes from Québec City)
- **Website:** www.atelierpare.com
- **Specialty:** Storytelling through wood sculpture—scenes from Québec folklore, legends, and rural life

Overview:
This folk art studio and gallery celebrates **traditional woodcarving**, with vivid sculptures that narrate Québecois myths, fairy tales, and daily farm life. A visual treat for families and fans of oral history.

Seasonal Art Events & Outdoor Exhibitions

- **Symposium de peinture de Baie-Saint-Paul** – A major art event in nearby Charlevoix, featuring live painting, lectures, and open-air exhibitions
- **Passages Insolites** – Annual public art circuit in Old Québec, with **large-scale sculptures and installations** placed in alleys, walls, and courtyards (summer)
- **Fête de la Culture (Journées de la Culture)** – Free access to dozens of galleries, studios, and cultural institutions every September across Québec

Tips for Art Lovers in Québec City

- **Local is king:** Look for tags like "Fabriqué au Québec" or "Artiste de la région" for authentic finds
- Many galleries offer **international shipping** and **certificate of authenticity** on purchase
- Some venues operate **seasonally** or by appointment—call ahead, especially for smaller studios
- Combine visits with local cafés and bookstores for an immersive cultural afternoon
- Don't miss **artist talks, vernissages (openings), or workshops**—great opportunities to meet Québec's creative minds directly

From classical oil paintings of the St. Lawrence to bold experimental pieces exploring identity and change, Québec City's art scene is alive with imagination and grounded in a deep sense of place. Whether displayed in stone-walled galleries, sleek modern studios, or festive open-air exhibits, the visual culture here is both timeless and strikingly new.

8.3 French-Canadian Heritage & Traditions

Québec City isn't just a French-speaking destination—it's the **cradle of French civilization in North America**. From its stone buildings and cobbled streets to the food on your plate and the music in the square, the city radiates a living culture born from centuries of perseverance, creativity, and community. The French-Canadian identity is woven through its language, Catholic roots, rural traditions, and strong sense of local pride, all of which continue to shape Québec's unique character today.

This section explores the deep-rooted **heritage and traditions** of French Canada as experienced in Québec City, highlighting the customs, institutions, and ways of life that make it truly distinct.

A Living Legacy: The French Language & Identity

Overview:
French is not just Québec's official language—it is the **heart of its cultural identity**.

Québec City was founded in 1608 by Samuel de Champlain, and over four centuries later, it remains one of the few places in the Americas where French culture thrives in daily life.

Traditions & Realities:

- **Québécois French** is a unique dialect, with rich slang, nasal vowels, and expressions drawn from old Norman and Breton roots.
- French remains central to education, media, government, and art, protected by **language laws like Bill 101**, which ensures French predominance in signage and services.
- Locals deeply value their language—visitors who greet with "Bonjour!" are warmly received.

Catholic Influence & Religious Heritage

Overview:
Catholicism was central to French-Canadian life for centuries. Though modern Québec is more secular today, its **religious heritage is visible in its architecture, festivals, and values**.

Key Landmarks:

- **Notre-Dame de Québec Basilica-Cathedral** – Founded in 1647, this is the oldest cathedral in North America north of Mexico and home to a Holy Door (one of only seven in the world).
- **Séminaire de Québec** – An active theological institution founded in 1663, located in the heart of Old Québec.
- **Chapelle des Ursulines** – A peaceful 18th-century chapel from the city's first religious teaching order.

Traditions:

- Catholic feasts and rituals—like **Saint-Jean-Baptiste Day**, **Christmas Mass**, and **La Chandeleur** (Candlemas)—influenced public life and seasonal rhythms.
- Many of Québec's **proverbs, names, and expressions** are rooted in Catholic culture (e.g., "sacres"—religious words used as expletives).

Folklore, Storytelling & Oral Traditions

Overview:
Long winters and isolated rural life gave rise to a rich **oral storytelling tradition**, passed down around fires, in kitchens, and at communal events. These stories often blend history, legend, and morality with humor or warning.

Popular Legends:

- **La Chasse-Galerie** – The "flying canoe" tale of voyageurs who make a pact with the devil to visit their loved ones
- **Le Bonhomme Sept-Heures** – A cautionary tale used to scare children into going to bed
- **Feu Follet** – Mischievous spirits or "will-o'-the-wisps" said to haunt dark forests and bogs

Where to Experience It:

- **Evening storytelling tours** in Old Québec
- **Theater and folklore festivals** in summer and fall
- **Atelier Paré** (in Sainte-Anne-de-Beaupré) – A folk art museum dedicated to visual storytelling through sculpture

Traditional Music & Dance

Overview:

French-Canadian music blends **Celtic, Breton, and Indigenous influences**, often featuring rhythmic foot tapping ("la podorythmie"), fiddles, accordions, and call-and-response singing.

Musical Traditions:

- **La chanson québécoise** – A modern continuation of folk themes, popularized by artists like **Félix Leclerc, Gilles Vigneault**, and **La Bottine Souriante**
- **Reels and jigs** – Rooted in Acadian and Métis rhythms
- **Circle dances and square dancing** – Still performed during traditional festivals and weddings

Where to Hear It:

- Live music at **folk festivals** like the Fête de la Nouvelle-France
- Street musicians in **Quartier Petit-Champlain**
- Intimate venues such as **Le Pôle Culturel du Monastère des Augustines**

Cuisine as Cultural Expression

Overview:

Food in Québec isn't just sustenance—it's a celebration of history and homegrown ingredients. Much of the province's cuisine grew from **rural French peasant traditions**, adapted to harsh winters and local resources.

Traditional Dishes:

- **Tourtière** – À spiced meat pie from Saguenay-Lac-Saint-Jean
- **Pouding chômeur** – A Depression-era dessert of cake baked in hot syrup
- **Cipaille (Sea Pie)** – A layered meat and pastry dish
- **Cretons** – A spiced pork pâté served at breakfast
- **Tire d'érable (Maple Taffy)** – Maple syrup poured on snow and rolled onto a stick

Where to Taste Tradition:

- **Aux Anciens Canadiens** – A historic home-turned-restaurant offering classic recipes
- **Traditional sugar shacks (cabane à sucre)** on **Île d'Orléans** or in the **Laurentians** during spring

- **Public markets** and festivals featuring regional specialties

Rural Traditions & the Spirit of Community

Overview:
Québec's deep connection to the land and rural life is at the heart of its identity. Farming, forestry, hunting, and fishing shaped both **seasonal traditions** and **values of self-reliance, generosity, and hospitality**.

Rural Customs:

- **"Veillées"** – Evening gatherings with music, storytelling, and shared meals
- **Harvest festivals and "vendanges"** (grape harvests) in wine regions like Île d'Orléans
- **Maple sugaring season (la saison des sucres)** – Celebrated with syrup production and communal meals
- **Cultural values of family, resilience, and pride in manual craft and labor**

Festivals Celebrating French-Canadian Identity

Fête de la Saint-Jean-Baptiste (June 24)

Québec's national holiday, a powerful symbol of **Francophone pride and cultural identity**. Celebrations include fireworks, music, parades, and massive outdoor concerts in Québec City.

Fêtes de la Nouvelle-France (Early August)

A living history festival in Old Québec where locals don 17th-century costumes, reenact colonial life, and honor the early settlers' legacy through food, music, and public performance.

Carnaval de Québec (Late January to early February)

Winter's biggest celebration showcases **ice canoe races, snow sculptures, and Bonhomme Carnaval**, blending tradition with festive flair.

Preserving the Heritage Today

Québecois culture is deeply resilient. Even in a modern, globalized world, its people continue to honor their **language, customs, and local art forms**, often weaving tradition into contemporary practice.

Modern Expressions of Heritage:

- **Francophone theater, literature, and film** addressing cultural themes
- **Cultural organizations and co-ops** that keep crafts, language, and music alive
- **Bilingual education**, with a strong foundation in history and pride

Tips for Experiencing French-Canadian Heritage in Québec City

- **Engage in French** when possible—even a simple "Bonjour!" makes a difference
- Visit **cultural centers, folk museums, and traditional festivals** to see living heritage
- Seek out **Québec-made food, art, and crafts**—they are windows into the past and present
- Respect the **quiet pride** of locals and their efforts to preserve identity amid change
- Attend **local mass or choir concerts** in historic churches for a sacred-cultural experience

From sacred rituals and rural folklore to maple feasts and fiddle dances, Québec City's French-Canadian heritage is not frozen in the past—it's a **vibrant part of everyday life**. In this city, history is lived, spoken, sung, and savored. Every stone, story, and song invites you to connect with a culture that is proudly unique, and undeniably alive.

Chapter 9. Shopping & Souvenirs

9.1 Best Shopping Streets & Local Markets

Shopping in Québec City isn't about big-box stores or generic souvenirs—it's about **authenticity**, **craftsmanship**, and **a deep sense of place**. From cobbled lanes lined with artisan boutiques to bustling public markets filled with fresh local produce, the city offers a vibrant shopping scene that's as rich in charm as it is in quality. Whether you're after gourmet goods, fine art, handwoven textiles, or keepsakes with cultural flair, these top shopping streets and local markets provide something for every traveler.

Rue du Petit-Champlain

- **Location:** Quartier Petit-Champlain, Lower Town (Basse-Ville)
- **Best For:** Artisanal crafts, jewelry, local art, and festive window shopping

Overview:
 Often called **North America's oldest shopping street**, Rue du Petit-Champlain is a fairytale-like pedestrian lane nestled beneath Cap Diamant. Lined with **stone**

buildings, colorful shutters, and lantern-lit windows, it's one of the city's most photogenic shopping areas.

What to Buy:

- Hand-painted silk scarves and leather goods
- Locally made maple products and gourmet treats
- Québecois fashion, winter accessories, and artisanal soap

Notable Shops:

- **Boutique Amimoc** – Authentic moccasins handmade in Québec
- **La Petite Cabane à Sucre** – Maple everything, from syrup to candies
- **Atelier Paré** – Folk art and wood carvings inspired by Québec legends

Seasonal Magic:

The street transforms during **winter holidays and summer festivals**, with twinkling lights, live performers, and themed decorations enhancing the shopping experience.

Rue Saint-Jean

- **Location:** From Old Québec to Saint-Roch
- **Best For:** Books, fashion, gourmet shops, indie boutiques

Overview:

Rue Saint-Jean is a dynamic boulevard that shifts in vibe as it moves from the fortified Old City into the modern, artistic Saint-Roch neighborhood. It's a **favorite among locals** for its unique shops and diverse eateries.

What to Explore:

- **Librairie Pantoute** – Québec's beloved independent French-language bookstore
- **Boutique Jupon Pressé** – Eclectic women's fashion and Québec-made accessories
- **Érico** – Chocolate museum, shop, and café offering handmade truffles

Tips:

- Look for **"Produit du Québec"** labels for locally sourced goods
- Side streets (like Rue Couillard) hide gems like bespoke tailors and vintage shops

Rue Saint-Paul

- **Location:** Old Port (Vieux-Port)
- **Best For:** Art galleries, antiques, Québec décor, and collectibles

Overview:

Rue Saint-Paul has a quieter, more refined atmosphere, drawing collectors and art lovers. Its 18th- and 19th-century architecture now houses **antique dealers, painters, and specialty shops**.

Highlights:

- **Antiquités Bolduc** – One of the city's oldest antique shops
- **Galerie Le Chien d'Or** – Fine art inspired by Québec's landscapes
- **Musical instrument boutiques and vintage map sellers** dot the area

Nearby Attraction:

The Old Port Market is just around the corner, making this a great spot for an afternoon of slow browsing and light shopping.

Grand Marché de Québec (Québec Public Market)

- **Location:** 250-M, Boulevard Wilfrid-Hamel, near ExpoCité
- **Website:** www.grandmarchedequebec.com
- **Hours:** Daily (varies by season), generally 9 AM – 6 PM

Overview:

This **modern, open-air style market** is the beating heart of Québec's food culture. It brings together more than **100 local producers and artisans** under one roof in a vibrant, spacious setting filled with sights, scents, and tastes.

Must-Try & Buy:

- Artisan cheeses, like Migneron or Riopelle
- Fresh bread, pastries, and wood-fired pizza
- Jams, ciders, herbal teas, craft beers, and micro-distilled gins
- Seasonal produce: strawberries (early summer), apples (fall), squash (autumn)

Features:

- Indoor food court and tasting bars
- Free parking and bike-friendly access
- Seasonal events, workshops, and children's activities

Pro Tip:
Visit in the morning for the best product selection, or later in the afternoon for relaxed browsing and casual snacking.

Marché du Vieux-Port (Old Port Market)

Note: Merged into the Grand Marché in 2019
While the original Old Port Market is no longer active as a standalone space, many of its **legacy vendors** and traditional producers are now part of the Grand Marché. However, the Old Port area still boasts seasonal pop-up markets, **outdoor Christmas fairs**, and summer **farmer stalls** along the riverwalk.

Avenue Cartier (Montcalm District)

- **Location:** Upper Town, near the Musée national des beaux-arts du Québec
- **Best For:** Boutique fashion, gifts, florists, gourmet items

Overview:
This **chic and artsy neighborhood** is dotted with independent stores, local cafés, and designer fashion houses. During the holidays, the street is lit with giant lamp shades printed with local artwork, making it one of the most atmospheric shopping areas in the city.

What to Look For:

- Fine perfumes, cosmetics, and Québec-made skincare
- Designer winterwear and handmade jewelry
- Artisan bakeries and chocolatiers

Place Royale & Surroundings

- **Location:** Lower Town near the waterfront
- **Best For:** Upscale souvenirs, historical reproductions, artisan gifts

Overview:
In the heart of colonial history, Place Royale blends **heritage with commerce**. While it's a major tourist hub, many of the boutiques here emphasize **high-quality handmade items** rooted in French and Indigenous tradition.

Top Picks:

- **Terroir Local** – High-end edible souvenirs like cider, foie gras, and sea buckthorn

- **Boutique Métiers d'Art** – Unique Québec-made crafts, pottery, and glass
- **Côté Est** – Home décor inspired by New France aesthetic

Tips for Shopping in Québec City

- **Tax refund for visitors:** If you're from outside Canada, ask for receipts and check eligibility for a **GST/HST rebate** on larger purchases
- **Look for "Artisanat du Québec" or "Fait au Québec"** to support local creators
- **Most boutique shops accept credit/debit cards**, but bring cash for markets or roadside stands
- **Pack extra space in your luggage**—especially for food items, art prints, and clothing
- **Best time to shop for deals:** Post-holiday January sales, summer clearance (July), and local artisan fairs during fall festivals

From charming alleyways filled with handcrafted treasures to grand public markets bursting with flavors, shopping in Québec City is about discovering **authentic stories through tangible items**. It's a joy for the senses—and a perfect way to take a piece of this historic and artistic city home with you.

9.2 Québec-Made Products & Crafts

Québec City is a treasure trove for travelers looking to bring home something meaningful, beautifully made, and uniquely rooted in local tradition. Whether it's a jar of hand-harvested maple butter, a woolen blanket from ancestral looms, or a piece of contemporary Indigenous beadwork, these **Québec-made products and crafts** reflect the province's deep heritage, vibrant creativity, and enduring connection to the land.

In this section, we explore the finest handcrafted goods and regional specialties worth discovering during your visit.

Maple Products (Produits d'Érable)

Overview:
Québec produces more than **70% of the world's maple syrup**, and the quality is second to none. But beyond the classic amber syrup, local producers offer an array of **innovative and gourmet maple creations**.

Must-Try Products:

- Pure maple syrup (grades: Golden, Amber, Dark, Very Dark)
- Maple sugar and maple taffy
- Maple butter (a creamy, spreadable delight)
- Maple-infused mustard, sauces, vinaigrettes
- Maple liqueurs and spirits

Where to Buy:

- **La Petite Cabane à Sucre** (Petit-Champlain)
- **Marché public Limoilou** and **Grand Marché de Québec**
- Farm shops on **Île d'Orléans**, especially in spring during the sugaring season

Handwoven Textiles & Wool Products

Overview:
Québec's cold winters gave rise to a strong tradition of textile artistry—blankets, shawls, and garments made from **locally sourced wool, linen, and cotton**, often woven on ancestral looms using techniques passed down through generations.

What to Look For:

- Wool socks, mittens, and tuques (knitted caps)
- Hand-loomed blankets and table runners
- Traditional "ceinture fléchée" (arrow sashes), iconic of French-Canadian identity

Top Artisan Sources:

- **Boutique Artisans Canada** (Place Royale)
- **Bilodeau Canada** – Known for fur-lined winterwear and accessories made in Saguenay
- **Wendake community shops** for Indigenous-style textiles with cultural patterns

Indigenous Arts & Crafts

Overview:

The Indigenous peoples of Québec—particularly the **Huron-Wendat, Innu, and Atikamekw Nations**—have rich artistic traditions grounded in the natural world, spirituality, and oral storytelling. Artworks are often both decorative and functional, reflecting deep cultural knowledge.

Common Handcrafted Items:

- Beaded jewelry and leather goods (moccasins, bags)
- Dreamcatchers, feathered ornaments
- Birchbark baskets, porcupine quill boxes
- Carvings in soapstone, wood, and antler

Where to Find Them:

- **Wendake Artisans' Market** (at the Huron-Wendat Traditional Site or La Boutique Wendake)
- **Maison Tsawenhohi**, Wendake
- Select stores in Petit-Champlain that feature Indigenous co-ops and fair-trade sourcing

Ceramics, Pottery & Glass Art

Overview:

Québec artisans have embraced ceramics as both an artistic medium and a traditional craft. The province's ceramic scene includes everything from **folk-style crockery** to **sleek, modern pieces** using local clay and natural glazes.

Noteworthy Items:

- Hand-painted ceramic bowls and espresso cups
- Glazed candle holders and pitchers
- Glass-blown ornaments and vases

Where to Shop:

- **Galerie Boutique Métiers d'Art** (Place Royale)
- **Galerie Québec Art** (Rue Saint-Paul)
- **Coopérative Le Pot** – Ceramists' collective in Old Limoilou

Leather Goods & Moccasins

Overview:
With deep roots in both French colonial and Indigenous traditions, Québec-made leather products combine durability with artistry. Handmade moccasins, belts, and wallets are especially popular for their craftsmanship and cultural resonance.

Top Picks:

- **Amimoc** – Premium moccasins made in Québec since 1956
- **Rudsa** – Local workshop producing high-end leather bags, belts, and accessories
- Leather-bound journals and artisan wallets in Rue Saint-Jean shops

Pro Tip:
Look for goods labeled **"fabriqué à la main au Québec"** to ensure authentic production.

Gourmet Québec Products

Overview:
The culinary scene in Québec is just as rich as its arts, and many local gourmet items make ideal edible souvenirs—**perfectly packaged, long-lasting, and deeply flavorful**.

Popular Selections:

- Artisan cheeses (Laiterie Charlevoix, Fromagerie des Grondines)
- Ciders and ice ciders (Côte-de-Beaupré, Île d'Orléans)
- Craft beers and gins (from Microbrasseries like Noctem and St-Pancrace)
- Wild berry jams, sea buckthorn products, and herbal teas

Best Sources:

- **Grand Marché de Québec**
- Farm shops and cider houses on **Route de la Nouvelle-France**
- **Aliments du Québec** logo on packaging ensures provincial origin

Wood Carvings & Folk Art

Overview:
Folk art in Québec is not only decorative—it's a form of storytelling. Traditional **wood carving**, rooted in rural and religious customs, remains a vibrant practice.

Signature Pieces:

- Sculptures of historic or religious figures
- Depictions of rural life: horses, carriages, log homes
- Painted signs, decorative panels, and nativity scenes

Where to Find:

- **Atelier Paré** (Sainte-Anne-de-Beaupré) – Specializes in mythological and narrative carvings
- **Rue Saint-Paul antique shops**
- **Seasonal Christmas markets** for collectible wooden ornaments

Québec Fashion & Jewelry Designers

Overview:
Québec has a strong independent fashion scene, with many designers emphasizing **sustainability, natural fabrics, and local sourcing**. Jewelry makers often work with **reclaimed wood, stone, and metal**, crafting minimalist or nature-inspired pieces.

Top Designers to Look For:

- **Annie 50** – Feminine fashion with vintage flair
- **Catherine C. Jewelry** – Nature motifs in silver and brass
- **Veinage** – Leather-and-wood bags and accessories handmade in Montréal

Where to Shop:

- **Jupon Pressé** (Rue Saint-Jean)

- **Simons La Maison** – Large department store with Québec fashion collections
- **Pop-up markets and local designer fairs** in summer and fall

Tips for Buying Local Products in Québec City

- **Ask for artist bios or certification cards**—many items come with creator details or heritage info
- **Avoid mass-produced souvenir shops**; instead, look for co-ops, galleries, or public markets
- For food gifts, confirm **airline/travel compliance** (especially with alcohol and dairy products)
- Many artisan boutiques offer **international shipping** or secure packing for transport
- Buying direct from **craftspeople and cooperatives** supports sustainable local economies

From intricate beadwork to maple-infused delicacies, Québec City's local products and crafts reflect a culture grounded in **tradition, quality, and storytelling**. They're more than souvenirs—they're keepsakes of a place where heritage and creativity are woven into everyday life.

9.3 Fashion, Boutiques & Antique Finds

Québec City offers a **distinctive and eclectic shopping experience** for those seeking stylish fashion, curated boutiques, and timeless antiques. The city's shopping landscape blends **Parisian elegance** with **Québécois creativity**, making it a haven for fashion lovers, vintage enthusiasts, and collectors alike. Whether you're after designer wear, handmade accessories, or historical treasures, Québec's fashion and antique districts deliver a shopping experience full of character and cultural flair.

Fashion & Designer Boutiques

Rue Saint-Jean & Saint-Roch District

- **Style:** Trendy, indie, eco-conscious, and Québécois-designed
- **Highlights:** Up-and-coming fashion labels, vintage-inspired pieces, bold accessories

Overview:
The streets of Saint-Jean and Saint-Roch are hubs for **fashion-forward locals**. Here, you'll find **independent fashion houses**, vintage shops, and eco-friendly brands that reflect the province's creative spirit and dedication to craftsmanship.

Notable Boutiques:

- **Jupon Pressé** (790 Rue Saint-Jean): Whimsical women's wear, retro-chic pieces, and accessories by Québec designers
- **Karkass** (Saint-Roch): Handcrafted leather bags and urban accessories with an industrial flair
- **Clémentine Boutique**: Minimalist designs, neutral tones, and sustainable materials for modern wardrobes
- **Article 721**: Carefully curated fashion-forward wear and accessories in a laid-back loft-style space

Pro Tip:
Explore Rue Saint-Joseph Est (in Saint-Roch) for **concept stores** and **limited-run designer items**, many made right in Québec.

Simons – La Maison Simons

- **Location:** 20 Côte de la Fabrique, near Place d'Armes (Old Québec)
- **Website:** www.simons.ca
- **Style:** Classic to contemporary, with a strong emphasis on local fashion and international brands

Overview:
Founded in Québec City in 1840, **Simons** is one of Canada's most iconic department stores. The flagship store blends timeless elegance with cutting-edge fashion, offering everything from **Québec designer lines** to **affordable casual wear**.

What to Shop For:

- Signature lines like **Twik, Contemporaine, Djab**, and **Icône**
- Homeware collections designed in-house
- Capsule collections from Québec-based designers and artists

Les Boudoirs de Mode & Artisan Jewelry

Best For: One-of-a-kind pieces, elegant accessories, and wearable art

Recommended Spots:

- **Anne-Marie Chagnon** – Sculptural jewelry with bronze, pewter, and glass (found in select boutiques)
- **Mademoiselle Fizz** – Bold fashion jewelry made with repurposed materials
- **Boutique Maniak** – Statement clothing and urban wear inspired by graffiti and punk design

Vintage & Secondhand Fashion

La Friperie Saint-Joseph

- **Location:** 250 Rue Saint-Joseph Est
- **Style:** Vintage, bohemian, recycled, and designer secondhand

Overview:
A vintage paradise in the artsy Saint-Roch district, this friperie (thrift boutique) offers a **well-curated selection** of secondhand garments, denim jackets, retro dresses, and accessories.

Look For:

- 1970s and 1980s fashion
- Denim, leather boots, and reworked vintage coats
- Vintage Québec-made labels

Trésor de Rue

- **Location:** Rue Saint-Jean area

- **Specialty:** Accessories, handbags, costume jewelry, and gently used vintage fashion

Antique Shopping & Collectibles

Rue Saint-Paul: Québec's Antique Row

- **Location:** Old Port district
- **Atmosphere:** Quiet, refined, heritage-laced street ideal for leisurely browsing

Overview:
Rue Saint-Paul is **Québec City's premier destination for antique lovers**, offering everything from **century-old furniture** and **fine china** to **religious icons**, maritime relics, and rare collectibles.

Top Antique Shops:

- **Antiquités Bolduc** – Established antique house featuring 18th and 19th-century Québecois furniture
- **Antiquités Jean-Pierre** – Specializes in fine porcelain, silverware, vintage maps, and framed etchings
- **Galerie Saint-Paul** – A blend of vintage art, sculpture, and collector's pieces from across Canada and Europe

What to Hunt For:

- **Folk art sculptures and religious figurines**
- **Old navigation instruments and compasses**
- **Early Canadian coins, stamps, and lithographs**

Tip:
Bring cash or be ready to negotiate—some shops offer discounts for multiple-item purchases or collectors.

Home Décor & Québec Design

Overview:
If you're seeking pieces that reflect Québec's unique aesthetic—think rustic elegance, French provincial charm, or minimalist northern design—local boutiques and studios specialize in furniture, handmade décor, and lifestyle accessories.

Where to Shop:

- **Côté Est** (Place Royale): Artisanal home décor and decorative antiques with a New France theme
- **L'Atelier du Presbytère** (Old Québec): Linen textiles, farmhouse-inspired ceramics, and repurposed antique materials
- **Zone Maison** (Avenue Cartier): Sleek modern home goods, kitchenware, and Québec-made interior design items

Fashion & Antique Shopping Tips

- **Sizes vary**: Try on clothing in-store; many Québec designers follow European sizing
- **Tax refund eligibility**: International visitors may qualify for sales tax refunds on larger purchases—ask for detailed receipts
- **Ask about origin**: Look for **"Conçu et fabriqué au Québec"** (Designed and made in Québec)
- **Antique transport**: Some antique dealers offer **shipping services**, especially for larger furniture or fragile art

From forward-thinking designer labels to timeless antiques steeped in French-Canadian heritage, Québec City is a **cultural shopping destination** where history and modernity walk hand in hand. Whether you're stepping into a sleek fashion boutique or browsing hand-carved heirlooms, you'll discover goods that are as storied and beautiful as the city itself.

Chapter 10. Travel Tips & Practical Information

10.1 Language, Currency & Tipping

Visiting Québec City is an experience steeped in culture, history, and hospitality—but to truly make the most of your journey, it's helpful to understand the **local customs, linguistic nuances, and everyday etiquette**. This section covers the basics: how to communicate, what to expect when paying, and how to tip respectfully and confidently.

Language: Bonjour! Bienvenue à Québec

Primary Language:

- **French** is the official language of Québec and is spoken by the vast majority of Québec City residents.
- While many locals in tourist areas speak **basic to fluent English**, especially in hotels, restaurants, and shops, **making an effort to speak French is appreciated** and often rewarded with warm hospitality.

Essential French Phrases to Know:

English	French
Hello / Good day	Bonjour
Please	S'il vous plaît
Thank you	Merci
Excuse me / Sorry	Excusez-moi / Désolé
Do you speak English?	Parlez-vous anglais ?
I don't understand	Je ne comprends pas
How much does it cost?	Combien ça coûte ?
Where is the bathroom?	Où sont les toilettes ?

Pro Tip:
Start every interaction with a cheerful **"Bonjour!"**—even if you immediately switch to English after. It's a small gesture that goes a long way in showing respect for the local culture.

Currency: The Canadian Dollar (CAD)

Currency Basics:

- Québec uses the **Canadian Dollar ($ CAD)**.
- Coins include: **5¢ (nickel), 10¢ (dime), 25¢ (quarter), $1 (loonie), and $2 (toonie)**
- Bills include: **$5, $10, $20, $50, and $100**, often color-coded and made of polymer (plastic) for durability.

Payment Methods:

- **Credit and debit cards** are widely accepted, including Visa, MasterCard, and Interac.
- Contactless payments (tap) are popular and fast.
- **Cash** is still useful for small purchases, street vendors, taxis, and some markets.

Currency Exchange & ATMs:

- **Currency exchange booths** are available at the airport, Gare du Palais (train station), and in the Old City.
- **ATMs (guichets)** are widely available in banks and convenience stores. Look for bank-affiliated machines for better rates.
- You can withdraw CAD using most international bank cards, but **transaction fees may apply**.

Pro Tips:

- Notify your bank before traveling to avoid blocked card usage.
- Avoid exchanging money at hotels or airports unless necessary—they often charge higher fees.
- Check real-time exchange rates to stay informed (mid-market rate is the most accurate).

Tipping Etiquette in Québec City

Tipping is a **firm part of Canadian culture**, and expected in many service settings. While gratuities are technically optional, they are **strongly customary and considered part of a service worker's income**.

General Tipping Guidelines:

Service	Suggested Tip
Restaurant Waitstaff	15% – 20% (pre-tax amount); more for exceptional service
Bar Service	**$1–$2 per drink**, or 15%–20% of the tab
Hotel Housekeeping	**$2–$5 per day**, left daily with a note
Concierge / Bellhop	$2–$5 depending on service (e.g., luggage help, reservations)
Taxi / Uber	10%–15%, or round up to the nearest dollar
Spa & Salon Services	15%–20% of the total bill

How to Tip:

- **On card payments:** Most card machines prompt you to add a tip percentage or dollar amount.

- **In cash:** Leave it on the table or hand it directly. It's polite to say "Merci!" when tipping.
- **In group settings:** Check the bill—**some restaurants include a gratuity (service compris)** for groups of 6 or more.

Pro Tip:

While tipping is expected, it's also an **opportunity to show appreciation** for friendly or attentive service—something Québec City is known for.

Other Practical Notes:

Sales Tax:

- Québec applies a **combined 14.975% tax** on most goods and services:
    - 5% **GST (federal)**
    - 9.975% **QST (provincial)**
- Sales tax is **not included in the listed price**, so be prepared for a higher total at checkout.

Receipts & Tax Refunds for Visitors:

- Canada no longer offers general sales tax refunds for tourists.
- However, if you're purchasing **large items to ship internationally**, ask vendors about **tax-exempt or duty-free options**.

Final Tips for Travelers

- **Bring a small phrasebook or translation app**—especially useful outside of tourist areas.
- **Be polite and patient**—even if there's a language barrier, most locals will try their best to assist you.
- **Watch out for different electrical outlets**—Canada uses 120V with Type A/B plugs (same as the U.S.).
- **No need to bargain**—haggling isn't common in Canadian shops or markets.

Whether you're ordering a café au lait in French or calculating a restaurant tip after a hearty Québécois meal, a little awareness of local practices can make your trip smoother and more enriching. Québec City is warm and welcoming—especially to those who come prepared with **respect and curiosity**.

10.2 Safety & Emergency Contacts

Québec City is often ranked as **one of the safest cities in North America**, offering a peaceful, well-organized, and welcoming environment for visitors. Still, being prepared with safety tips and knowing who to contact in case of an emergency is essential for a stress-free travel experience. This section covers **personal safety, health preparedness, local emergency services**, and key contact information you should keep handy during your stay.

General Safety Overview

Crime & Personal Security:

- **Very low crime rate**—violent crime is rare, and most areas are safe to explore even after dark.
- **Petty theft**, such as pickpocketing or unattended bag theft, is rare but can occur in crowded tourist areas—particularly in the Old City, during festivals, or on public transit.
- Locals are known for being **friendly, polite, and helpful**, and tourist-targeted scams are uncommon.

Safe Neighborhoods for Tourists:

- **Old Québec (Vieux-Québec)** – Safe day and night, with high tourist presence and well-lit streets.
- **Montcalm, Saint-Roch & Saint-Jean-Baptiste** – Popular with travelers, students, and families.
- **Limoilou & Lebourgneuf** – Residential and calm, ideal for long stays or local experiences.

Night Safety Tips:

- Use common sense: stick to well-lit streets, especially in less-trafficked parts of the Lower Town after dark.
- Avoid walking alone in unfamiliar wooded areas or alleys late at night.
- Taxis and rideshares (Uber) are safe and reliable at all hours.

Health & Medical Services

Health Care Access:

- Canada has a public health care system, but **non-residents must pay out of pocket** or have **travel insurance** for medical care.
- Québec City has **modern hospitals, emergency clinics, and pharmacies**, many with bilingual staff.

Major Hospitals:

1. **CHU de Québec – Hôpital de l'Enfant-Jésus**

   - *Address:* 1401 18e Rue, Québec, QC G1J 1Z4
   - *Phone:* +1 418-649-0252
   - *Services:* Trauma, emergency, general medicine, surgery

2. **CHU de Québec – Hôpital Saint-François d'Assise**

   - *Address:* 10 Rue de l'Espinay, Québec, QC G1L 3L5
   - *Phone:* +1 418-525-4444

3. **Centre Médical Saint-Louis** *(for minor emergencies)*

   - *Address:* 8020 Boulevard Henri-Bourassa, Québec, QC
   - *Website:* www.centremedicalstlouis.com

Pharmacies:

- **Jean Coutu, Pharmaprix (Shoppers Drug Mart),** and **Familiprix** are Québec's main pharmacy chains.
- Pharmacists can **offer consultations**, refill prescriptions, and recommend over-the-counter remedies.

Emergency Numbers (Québec City & Canada-Wide)

Situation	Number	Notes
All Emergencies (Police, Fire, Ambulance)	911	Available 24/7; French and English service
Non-Urgent Police Assistance (Service de police de la Ville de Québec – SPVQ)	+1 418-641-6111	For reports, minor incidents
Québec City Info & Services (311)	311	City services, snow removal, road closures
Québec Poison Control Centre (Centre antipoison du Québec)	+1 800-463-5060	Immediate advice for poisoning or exposure
Tourist Assistance (Bonjour Québec)	+1 877-266-5687	Multilingual support for visitors

Embassies & Consulates:

Québec City has limited consular presence; however, **most foreign embassies are in Ottawa or Montréal.**

In case of lost passport or legal issues:

- Contact your nearest embassy or consulate in **Montréal**.
- U.S. Consulate General: +1 514-398-9695
- UK Consulate: +1 514-866-5863
- Nigerian High Commission (Ottawa): +1 613-236-0521

Weather-Related & Seasonal Safety

Winter Travel Safety:

- **Snow & ice** can make sidewalks slippery—wear good boots with tread and use handrails.
- Dress in **layers, windproof outerwear, gloves, and hats** during cold months (Nov–March).
- **Black ice** is common on roads and walkways; take extra care when driving or walking.

Summer Weather Cautions:

- Québec summers are generally mild, but **heatwaves** occasionally occur (30°C+ / 86°F+).
- Carry water, wear sunscreen, and **stay shaded** during peak sun hours.
- **Insects (mosquitoes & black flies)** are present in nature parks—use repellent if hiking.

Emergency Alerts:

- Québec uses the **Alert Ready system** to issue emergency warnings (e.g., severe storms, Amber Alerts) via mobile, TV, and radio.
- Download **MétéoMédia** or **The Weather Network app** for real-time weather updates.

COVID-19 & Health Precautions (as applicable)

- No current travel restrictions as of 2025, but travelers are advised to **stay updated** via:
    - www.quebec.ca/en – official government site for health measures
    - travel.gc.ca – for Canada-wide travel advisories
- **Masks and sanitizers** are optional in most public spaces but still recommended in crowded areas.

Travel Safety Tips at a Glance:

- **Carry ID and insurance info** at all times.
- **Use ATMs** in well-lit, secure areas (preferably inside banks).
- **Avoid flashing cash or expensive items** in crowded areas.

- **Save emergency contacts** in your phone and keep a written backup in your bag or wallet.
- **Obey traffic signals** when walking—jaywalking can result in fines.
- **Dial 911** immediately in any life-threatening situation or if you feel unsafe.

Final Word

Québec City is an exceptionally safe and well-serviced destination where most visitors enjoy trouble-free trips. Still, being informed and prepared ensures **peace of mind**. Whether it's icy sidewalks, a sudden flu, or an urgent passport issue, help is close by—and often just a **polite conversation away**.

10.3 Budgeting & Connectivity

Whether you're traveling on a tight schedule or indulging in a longer stay, understanding the **cost of travel in Québec City**, along with your **connectivity options**, helps you plan wisely, avoid surprises, and stay effortlessly connected. This section provides a full overview of **daily travel costs, money-saving tips**, and the best ways to **access Wi-Fi, mobile service, and digital tools** while exploring the city.

Budgeting for Your Trip

Typical Daily Costs (Per Person):

Budget Type	Daily Estimate (CAD)	Inclusions
Budget Traveler	$60–$100	Hostel, public transport, casual meals
Mid-Range Traveler	$150–$250	3-star hotel or B&B, attractions, restaurants
Luxury Traveler	$300+	Boutique/luxury hotel, fine dining, private tours

Cost Breakdown by Category

Accommodation:

- **Hostels & budget lodgings:** $30–$80/night
- **Mid-range hotels & inns:** $120–$220/night
- **Luxury hotels & boutique stays:** $250–$500+/night
- **Apartment rentals (Airbnb/VRBO):** $100–$200+/night depending on location and season

Food & Dining:

- **Quick bites (bakeries, poutine, crêperies):** $5–$15
- **Casual dining & bistros:** $15–$30 per meal
- **Fine dining experiences:** $50–$120+ per person (excluding wine)
- **Groceries (1–2 days' worth):** $25–$40 for basic items

Transportation:

- **Public transit (RTC buses):** $3.75 per single ride / $9.50 for 1-day unlimited pass
- **Taxi/Uber rides:** $10–$25 for short city trips
- **Bike rentals:** $10–$20/hour or $30–$50/day
- **Car rentals:** $50–$100/day (plus insurance & fuel)

Attractions & Activities:

- Many historical sites and churches are **free or donation-based**
- Museums: $10–$20 per adult entry
- Festivals & outdoor shows: Often **free or low-cost**
- Guided walking tours: $20–$40
- Day tours (e.g., to Île d'Orléans or Le Massif): $75–$150 per person

Money-Saving Tips

- **Get a Québec City Museum Pass**: Save on admission to multiple attractions over 3 days.
- **Use day passes on public transport**: Great value if you're hopping between neighborhoods.
- **Dine at lunch instead of dinner**: Many restaurants offer prix-fixe midday menus.
- **Visit local markets**: Fresh produce, snacks, and baked goods at lower prices than restaurants.
- **Travel during shoulder seasons** (May–June, Sept–Oct): Lower hotel rates and fewer crowds.
- **Stay in Limoilou or Montcalm**: More affordable than Old Québec with easy access via bus.

Staying Connected: Internet & Mobile Access

Wi-Fi Access:

- **Free Wi-Fi** is widely available in:
    - Hotels, cafés, restaurants, and museums
    - Public libraries and some public transport hubs
    - Old Québec's **Place D'Youville** and **Parliament Hill** areas
- **City-run Wi-Fi:** Look for networks such as **"ZAP Québec"**, a community Wi-Fi service

SIM Cards & Mobile Service:

Provider	Price (Prepaid SIM)	Coverage & Notes
Fido	$15–$50+	Great tourist plans, English support
Bell/Virgin Mobile	$30–$70+	Reliable coverage, includes data

Telus	$35–$75+	Strong network, available at kiosks
Public Mobile / Lucky Mobile	$15–$40	Budget options, online purchase recommended

- Most SIM cards are **available at major malls, convenience stores**, and mobile kiosks.
- Make sure your phone is **unlocked** before buying a Canadian SIM.

Roaming & International Travelers

- U.S. travelers may use **North America roaming plans**, but fees vary—check with your carrier before arrival.
- European and African travelers should consider **local SIMs or eSIM providers** for better data rates.
- For short stays, **portable Wi-Fi routers (MiFi)** or **eSIM data plans** (via apps like Airalo or Holafly) are ideal.

Helpful Travel Apps

Purpose	Recommended Apps
Transit schedules & real-time buses	RTC Nomade, Transit App
Weather updates	MétéoMédia, The Weather Network
Translation & language help	Google Translate (with French downloaded)
Navigation	Google Maps, Maps.me
Dining & reviews	Yelp, TripAdvisor, RestoQuebec
Event listings	Bonjour Québec, Eventbrite
Budgeting	Trail Wallet, XE Currency Converter

Final Tips for Budgeting & Staying Connected

- **Set a daily spending cap** to avoid overspending—factor in taxes and tips.
- **Keep some cash on hand** for tips, small vendors, and occasional tech-free moments.

- Always have **offline maps and translations** downloaded in case of weak signals.
- Québec is **card-friendly**, but rural areas and local markets may prefer cash.

From boutique hotels to back-alley bakeries, Québec City offers options for **every wallet and travel style**. By planning your budget wisely and staying digitally connected, you'll be able to experience the city with ease and confidence.

Would you like to continue with **10.4 Accessibility, Permits & Family Travel**, or head to the next chapter of your guide?

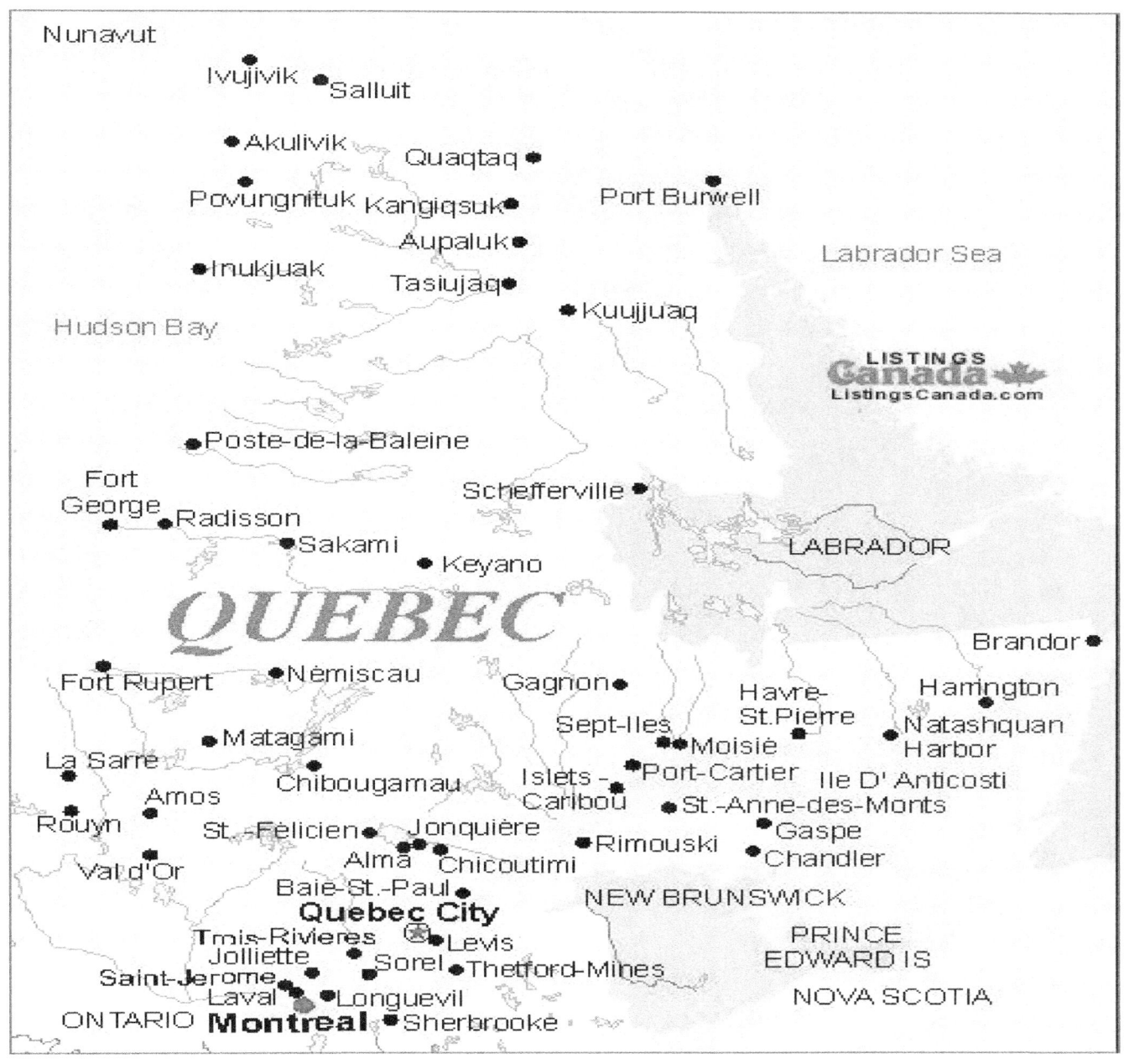

Printed in Dunstable, United Kingdom

77381552R00087